POCKET FULL OF
Quarters

Five Steps to
Loving God

CHERYLE M. TOUCHTON

A Division of WINEPRESS PUBLISHING

Pleasant Word (a division of WinePress Publishing, PO Box 428, Enumclaw, WA 98022) functions only as book publisher. As such, the ultimate design, content, editorial accuracy, and views expressed or implied in this work are those of the author.

ISBN 1-4141-0053-1
Library of Congress Catalog Card Number: 2005902675

Dedication

This book is lovingly dedicated to my husband Bob, daughter Kelley, son Chris, daughter-in-law Whitney, friends Nancy and Judy, and "my 4 parents" Mama, Daddy, Aunt Ka Ka, and Uncle Bobby. Their unfailing prayer, love, support, and confidence made this book possible. Special thanks goes to my nephew Bill for pushing me to finish and Michelle LaMontagne for superb editorial support.

Contents

Prologue

Dear God,   April 2

Last week I worked seventy hours and touched down in seven airports. Where do I find time for You or my family? This cannot be Your will, but I see no other choices. No matter how hard we work, the technology industry just keeps declining. Telling people they no longer have a job breaks my heart. Slowing down could result in more company layoffs. Is my love for work, people, and perhaps even the large salary getting in the way of hearing You? God, I offer myself to You, to do as You will.

Dear God,   April 3

My monthly prayer group is praying for Your will. Together, we asked You to do whatever it takes to help me find Your will at my company. I surrender my life, work, salary, and employees.

Oh God,   April 26

What happened? How did *my name* get on the layoff list? I closed a deal this morning that paid my salary for 2 years. Wasn't I reaching their goals? People warned about this possibility when I sold my company. Should I have listened? How can I face people? The house is filled with flowers from people who understand how broken I am. It feels like someone died. I have spent the last seventeen years of my life employing family and friends. What will I do tomorrow morning?

Dear Abba,   May 3

Where are You? My soul cries out in pain, and I find no respite. I have no strength because tears have exhausted me. I cannot make sense out of what happened. It seems unfair. How do I pray, *Father, forgive them. They know not what they do?*

OK God,   May 7

I spent the last ten days crying. Last night, the prayer group firmly reminded me of our recent prayer for Your will. Suddenly, I understood. Sorry it took so long. Your answer to our prayer was my layoff. Just for the record, this was not what I was looking for. The group says to praise You and I am trying. I guess I need to stop whining and ask what You want me to do next.

Oh God,   May 11

What? Are you really suggesting I take a journey across America and talk to people about God? Can I be hearing correctly? Shouldn't I be looking for a job?

But God,   May 12

This may be my daughter's last summer at home. What about Bob? In thirty years, we have never been apart for longer than a week. He reminded me that I have always dreamed of this, and he thinks You are speaking through my longings. He advised listening, but I am afraid. Why is my husband more confident in my ability to hear You than I am?

But God,   May 13

Mama is worried about this trip. Isn't worrying my mother breaking some kind of commandment? My best friend, Nancy, thinks someone with duct tape is going to murder me. Will You keep me safe?

But God,   May 14

Have I mentioned that getting ready for this trip is a lot of work? What about money? Remember the part about just losing my job? Someone suggested camping to save money. Surely, You remember that I have not slept in a tent since Girl Scouts. Someone else suggested cooking my own food. Have You tasted my cooking?

Dear God,   May 15

OK. You win. I really do love You and want to obey. My mind is clear now. I trust You to keep me safe, even from my own cooking. I will go where You want me to go. I offer my broken heart and wounded soul in service. I already feel stronger as Your strength becomes mine.

Dear God,   May 18

This is getting exciting. Bob and my former co-workers are building a website to post the adventures. You gave me the name—Pocket Full of Quarters—years ago when sharing quarters with others helped me find my spiritual gift for sharing your love with people around me. I'm having business cards made with www.pocketfullofquarters.com on it, so people can find the website. Someone suggested putting a real quarter in the card. Cool idea.

My poor black Suburban is sagging from the weight of the gear. Friends and family have covered the giant map in the kitchen with colored arrows. Why do I suspect You have Your own set of arrows for me? Bob insists I need something called a Global Positioning System. He actually believes I can learn how to use it. I think I should learn how to change a tire. Oh well, no time for that now.

Dear God,   May 22

Today is the day. I can't believe I am leaving home for months. Thank You for the Frequent Flier Points, so Bob can at least visit occasionally. I hope You don't expect me to post those romantic adventures on the website. Early this morning, Bob knelt by my chair and prayed with me. We held each other and cried. Please honor his faith by bringing me home safely. Give me Your love for my neighbors as I listen to their stories. Help me to listen with Your heart. Give me Your words when I talk. Remove anything that gets in the way of fully loving You. Direct my journey. Thank you for this great honor.

Love,
Cheryle

P.S. Are you sure I can pitch a tent? Why do Bob and You have so much confidence in me?

Based on the excerpts from the prayer journal of Cheryle M. Touchton

Introduction: Secrets of the Sh'ma

Don't you just love being on the inside of a secret? Getting the *down-low* as my daughter says it. How about the intrigue of hidden codes and messages? The secret we will be talking about as we start our journey across America is the *Sh'ma*. The word is pronounced *shema*, with a short *e* and the accent on the second syllable. If this is a new term to you, I need to warn you that the *Sh'ma* is important enough for our Jewish brethren to routinely memorize it. Many carry a miniature copy in a vial on a chain around their neck. Intrigued? Now, you too can benefit from the secrets of the *Sh'ma*.

But alas, the secrets we are talking about are hidden in plain view. God tells us throughout the Bible that we are to love Him and our neighbors. He then proceeds to tell us exactly *how* to do it. *Sh'ma* is a Hebrew word that actually means *to hear*. In Mark 12:29-31, Jesus repeats part of the *Sh'ma* and tells us this is the most important commandment:

> And Jesus answered him, The first of all the commandments is, Hear, O Israel; The Lord our God is one Lord: And thou shalt love the Lord thy God with all thy heart, and with all thy soul, and with all thy mind, and with all thy strength: this is the first commandment. And the second is like, namely this, Thou shalt love thy neighbour as thyself. There is none other commandment greater than these.
>
> (Mark 12:29-31 KJV)

God called me to travel America, talking and listening to the people of our glorious country. He has blessed me to be able to visit all fifty states, sleeping in tents, people's homes, and hotels. Thankfully, I have now graduated from a tent to a 1992 camper van. My call is to listen, encourage, teach, and evangelize.

God began preparing for Pocket Full of Quarters years ago when I had several family members grow critically ill over a few months. I spent extended time in ICU waiting rooms. In each situation, the outcome was losing a loved one.

ICU waiting rooms are a sub-culture where people depend heavily on others. People talk to each other. They minister and pray with strangers. Family, friends, and church members visit and meet needs spiritually, physically, and emotionally. Often they minister to others in that same waiting room. In those rooms, we became willing to do almost anything for each other. We prayed, cried, and laughed together. We cheered when the news was good and grieved when the news was bad.

One surprising need we all had was for quarters. We needed quarters to call family members with medical updates. Vending machines with needed food and drinks only took quarters. Our physical lives began revolving around quarters.

We constantly asked each other for quarters. We were willing to help with almost anything except giving away the coveted quarter. Most would part with them, but usually begrudgingly. Cafeteria visits included requests for quarters. If we found quarters, we were careful not to jingle our pockets and give the secret away.

I mentioned the need for quarters to my minister, Dr. Sam Wilson. On his next visit, he arrived with a roll of quarters. Suddenly I had a "Pocket Full of Quarters." I had enough to share. I laid these quarters out on a table. People used them as needed. When they came back from the cafeteria, they dumped their quarters into the stack. Sam's gift grew, and we all had a "Pocket Full of Quarters."

The last night I was there, only two patients were in ICU. My grandfather had experienced a serious heart attack. The other patient was the father of a young woman I befriended while swapping quarters. Around midnight, we heard a code called over the loud speaker. Crash carts noisily rushed down the hall. The ICU door flew open. My grandmother and the wife of the other patient were engrossed in dialogue and missed the commotion. The daughter and I knew that one of us was about to receive seemingly unbearable news.

We looked at each other, quietly stepped into the hall, and went to the door. People were running in and out. "Get out of the way!" a nurse demanded. Not wanting to return to the waiting room and face our relatives, together we stepped inside the phone booth where we had spent so many of those quarters.

Space was close, and we grew self-conscious. One of us whispered, "Let's pray." We collapsed into each other's arms. "God, give us strength to face what is about to happen. Help the wife of the person about to receive the worst news of her life. Give us your words of comfort." We felt God's peace in that phone booth. With tears rolling down our faces, we straightened. We were prepared to face our future. The ICU door slowly opened, and the nurse walked towards me. God used those quarters to pave the way. I walked back to the waiting room to find my grandmother.

Pocket Full of Quarters became my metaphor for being prepared for life. The lessons I learned in that ICU waiting room prepared me for my future. My relationship with God grew closer as I began spending more time with Him. As my pockets grew fuller, I began noticing the pain of the people around me and longed for them to have a pocket full of quarters too. As I traveled with my job, I began talking to people everywhere about their relationship with God. I prayed for opportunities to share the love of Christ, and I was astounded by the doors God opened. I longed to spend more time with people and to share these experiences with others, but the time constraints of my high-profile executive job kept me from it. When the technology industry collapsed in 2001, and I lost my executive position, my husband and I knew God had paved the way for me to fulfill God's call.

As I travel across the country, I listen to people's stories, talk about their relationship with God, get permission to write their story, and hand them a card with the address of the Pocket Full of Quarters website and my e-mail. These cards have a slot that holds a real quarter. Some try to return the quarter, but I refuse. I want them to have a pocket full of quarters. These free quarters are a symbol of God's free grace available to everyone. The quarter also helps them remember the name of the website where many go as a follow up to our conversation. Some e-mail me that they keep the quarter as a reminder of God's love.

People and churches open their hearts and homes as they share their spiritual stories and whisper their secrets. Most report that they believe in God. Many worship and some even serve Him diligently. Unfortunately, I also see many sagging shoulders and pain-filled eyes.

Most Believe

Statistics say that as many as 95% of Americans believe in a higher power. I believe the statistic because almost everyone told me they believed in something grander than humanity. A man that reported "I am he, and he is me" may have made it into the 95% statistic, but I had a relative who talked like that, and she was locked up for her own protection.

Many Worship

Many Americans worship God in a formal setting. I visited Christian churches of various sizes, denominations, races, and cultures filled with people striving to worship God in a multitude of ways. These Americans wake up on Sunday morning, dress in stylish clothes, and drive to a church where they spend an hour or more worshiping.

The variety of ways I experienced formal worship in America was invigorating. Some clapped and raised hands. Others stood like soldiers. Some used music. Some didn't. I experienced chanting, unison reading, and kneeling. Tools for worship included fire, streamers, tambourines, keyboards, candles, bells, incense, PowerPoint slides, hats, other musical instruments, and even a pet.

Some used wine for Eucharist, and others grape juice. Some danced. Others prayed for those who did. Some worshiped for hours while others dismissed at exactly sixty minutes. Perhaps the most surprising was the similarity of the message. The Holy Bible was used everywhere. The message of love from God the Father, Son, and Holy Spirit was astoundingly consistent.

Even people who didn't attend an organized church often said they worshiped in their own way. I met people who used nature, crystals, candles, and incense to worship some kind of god of their understanding. Few said they didn't worship.

Some Serve

Some people were working hard to serve God. I met preachers, teachers, cooks, artists, musicians, carpenters, business people, and others intent on serving God. Their service to God, their church, and the world was inspiring.

Few Love

I grew more concerned about people as each day passed. Few found joy from loving God above all else. Many serving God were exhausted. They wondered if they had pleased God. They wondered if they had done enough. Christians admitted to struggling with their relationship with Him. Wistful, they described a time when their love for God transcended all circumstances. Now, their backs were bent from the weight of their burdens.

I was halfway through my first journey across America when I realized that the *Sh'ma* is the secret to everything I had witnessed. Only a few people had found the secret formula for the abundant life promised in the Bible. These had stopped working on their problems to focus on loving God. His joy radiated from their eyes as they told their stories.

The word of God is the authority for this book. I studied the spiritual experiences of the twelve disciples and other Biblical followers of God, looking for relevance to the manifestation of the *Sh'ma* in the lives of Americans. Excitedly, I found the following repeated pattern:

Step One: Follow God, mind to Mind

Step One is to love God with our minds. Loving God begins with a decision. The ancients believed thoughts came from the heart. We moderns now know we make decisions with our mind. Regardless of where those thoughts come from, we are to link our thoughts to the thoughts of God, mind to Mind.

The disciples made a decision to say yes to Jesus before they fully understood what it meant to follow Him. It was an intellectual decision based on His request to them and His impact on them personally. They might have rethought their decision if they had known their *yes* would mean ridicule, pain, and death.

At first, there was discernible harshness in the ministry of the disciples, demonstrated in events like trying to keep children from Jesus. They fought over who would sit next to Jesus on His throne, and they judged the people around them. To their credit, they listened to Jesus and did as He asked, even when they did not understand. They grew spiritually and gave Him their best. Over time, their efforts resulted in the awakening of their emotions.

Step Two: Please God, heart to Heart

Next, we learn to love God with our hearts. The ancients believed emotions lived in the bowels, hence the term, *gut reaction*. We moderns believe (at least on Valentine's Day), that emotions come from the heart. Using the modern definition of *heart*, we please God when our emotions blend with His, heart to Heart.

Gradually the disciples fell in love with Jesus with what we would refer to as their hearts. Their emotions engaged as they began to see His impact on the world. This joined their heart to His. Their actions softened as their commitment to Him grew. We see Jesus scolding and teaching through their volatile emotions—like anger—as when Peter cut off the ear of a soldier who was harming his beloved Jesus. Never were their emotions engaged more than when the cross broke their hearts. Like us, those broken hearts temporarily paralyzed them.

Unfortunately, emotional love was not enough. After Jesus died, the disciples scattered in fear. They trembled behind locked doors, hiding their association with Jesus. These same people later changed the world. What made the difference? The rest of the *Sh'ma*.

Step Three: Embrace God, soul to Soul

Our soul is our essence, the core of who we are. When we accept Christ, the Holy Spirit joins our essence in eternal communion. How much of that essence we offer is entirely up to us. To love God with our entire soul, we must embrace Him, soul to Soul. Step Three is learning to love with our entire soul.

After the resurrection, the recognition of the divine aroused the disciples' souls as their understanding of the cross grew in the light of the resurrection. When Jesus left them with the Holy Spirit, the marked change in them became a witness for all time. Their ability to communicate with Jesus soul to Soul allowed Jesus to replace their essence with His. They lost focus on earthly existence and developed an eternal perspective as their relationship with Him grew closer than when He walked on earth.

Step Four: Serve God, strength by Strength

After we embrace God, His strength can become ours. Like the two tiny fish Jesus used to feed five-thousand people, our strength stretches and allows us to work tirelessly for God. We love God with our entire strength when we surrender our strength to His and serve Him, strength by Strength. Step Four in loving God is to love Him with our entire strength.

When Jesus died, He left an exhausted and emotionally depleted cluster of disciples. When He ascended into heaven, He left them energized. What was the difference? Their souls had met Jesus through the Holy Spirit. This tiny circle of disciples grew rapidly as they worked tirelessly to advance the cause of Christ. They built churches, fought political constraints, and traveled in perilous regions. They led people to Christ, working with strength far beyond human abilities.

Step Five: Love God's Children, neighbor to neighbor

The ability to love our neighbors as ourselves only comes after we fully love God with our thoughts, emotions, essence, and strength. We become willing to sacrifice anything to serve the people of this world and to show them the way to the next. With our entire being, we love God's children, neighbor to neighbor. The final step in being prepared to face life is to love our neighbors as ourselves.

Shortly after Jesus died on the cross, loving their neighbors was the last thing on the disciples' minds. Self-preservation was number one. As they matured through the stages of loving God with their mind, heart, soul, and strength, their love for their neighbors developed. The final stage of their growth was willingness to die for the world around them. At full maturity, they were fully prepared to face the challenges of their world.

Let me invite you to turn the page and discover the secrets of the *Sh'ma*. Together we shall meet people, visit churches, and have adventures. We'll have mountaintop experiences and use God's word to satisfy our spiritual appetites. The Holy Spirit will be our guide, and the Bible will be our map, so we will not get lost. Our starting point will be where we are now and our destination will be who God would have us to become. Together, we shall learn to love God more, one day at a time.

STEP ONE

Follow God, mind to Mind

And thou shalt love the Lord thy God with all thy mind.

(Mark 12:30 KJV)

*H*ave you made the intellectual decision to follow God?" I ask this question continually as I briefly explain, "I'm traveling across America, visiting churches, meeting people, and hearing their spiritual stories." Surprisingly, almost no one seems offended by the question.

One man said, "Everyone in my country is a Christian." *I want to live in that country!* After hearing the Biblical definition of Christianity, he was not so sure that everyone really was a Christian. Oh well. *So much for my dreams of Utopia.*

I began to realize that most people had an intellectual belief in a Creator. Their intellect told them there had to be a god. A vast majority of people were even willing to call the Creator by the name God. One man said that the world was entirely too orderly not to be planned. "I am too intelligent not to believe in God," another reported.

A young couple held hands and stood too close to the edge of Lover's Leap. The woman exclaimed, "How could anyone look at this view and not believe?" I wanted to scream, "Don't do it! Don't jump. You're too young to die!"

Even non-believers usually admit to evidence being strongly in favor of there being a higher design. I met a woman as we stood at the base of a sheer cliff, watching her husband and only son risk their lives by climbing the cliff, for the sake of recreation. "This is their second time," she said. "I joined them their first time, and I'll never do it again. I don't get it." I agreed and asked if she was praying for them. "Oh, I don't believe in God," she said matter-of-factly. "I guess you could say that I'm an agnostic."

"What do you mean by agnostic?" I asked.

"I'm just not sure there is any proof that there is a God." As her beloved family struggled to get to the next level of the cliff, she joked, "But feel free to pray for them."

I realized that in her fear, her thoughts had turned to God. "A-ha," I quipped, "so you do admit there might be Someone to pray to." That led to a long discussion about God, Jesus, and the Holy Spirit. After hearing her intellectual reasons for non-belief, I asked if she experienced restlessness. She admitted she did.

"I sometimes wonder what's wrong with me. I have everything I need." In listening to her life, I agreed. She is living the American Dream.

"Where do you go when you're seeking answers to problems?" I asked.

"Books, family, friends, and counseling," was the expected reply.

"Do they help?" I probed.

"Sometimes."

"What if God is the answer to your restlessness? What if believing in Him is the only way to peace? If you suspected that, would you be willing to seek Him?" She grew quiet and finally admitted she had never intellectually opened the door to a belief in God. "At least, take a look," I beseeched. "Ask the God you don't believe in to reveal Himself."

People enjoy talking about human relationships and giving opinions about God. They are less comfortable talking about a relationship with God. When discussing children, spouse, or friends, voices grow animated with emotion—positive and negative. When asked about a relationship with God, most stand straighter, stare off in the distance, and give intellectual answers.

I asked one woman about her relationship with God. "God is much bigger than Christianity, Buddhism, or Judaism," she said, dodging the question.

There is certainly no shortage of opinions about God:

- "He came to earth and died for my sins." Often words to very familiar hymns came to my mind. I resisted the urge to request a solo.
- "God has many names." They drew *names* out with the pitch falling off at the end. Usually I would prompt, "By what name do you call Him?"
- Another very popular answer was, "I am spiritual but not religious." When asked the definitions, spiritual included love, peace, joy, and the ability to do whatever they wished. Religion was boring, judgmental, and evil. Webster certainly does not agree with those definitions.
- Many would brag, "I am active in my church," or "I read the Bible continually." I usually resisted the urge to get competitive.
- Some smugly said, "God is for people who need a crutch." My retort to that is, "I prefer to call them wings."
- "I have given up on formal religion," would be accompanied by a head toss.
- "My parents go to church," indicated they were more enlightened than their parents.
- "I was raised in church but no longer go," was usually followed by a guilty "tsk" or silent headshake.
- When I heard, "God is in the universe, wind, mountains, or (fill in the blank)," I would wait and, sure enough, they would look around.
- I was surprised at how many people grouped Gandhi, Jesus, Mohamed, and Moses into one category. I sensed an air of intellectual superiority in the people that told me, "We have something to learn from all of them."

Our minds can get us into trouble if we let them. In general, I try to avoid intellectual debates because I know they solve very little. Besides, I am lousy at debating and hate losing. Having said that, I could not resist asking one woman, "Why would you be willing to learn from a liar?" She had just told me that Jesus was not the Messiah but He could teach us a lot. I felt a still small voice whispering, "Stop now, you are getting in over your head." Instead, I proceeded.

"Jesus said He was the one true Son of God. If He isn't, then He must be a liar. Why would you think a liar has a lot to teach us?" Suddenly, I had set us up as opponents. She happily sighed and launched into her well-prepared debate answers. As usual, I could not keep up. She enjoyed the conversation, but I had blown it.

I did not learn anything about her or her heart, only her opinions. We left the conversation with her knowing only my intellectual opinions about God and nothing about my tender and personal relationship with Him. I apologized to God for giving in to the temptation to match intellectual wits. I tried to apologize to her, but that led to a debate about the necessity of an apology.

If you are a Christian, don't feel too smug. The most popular answer was, "I am a Catholic," (or Baptist, Presbyterian, non-denominational…). I would laugh and ask a second time about their relationship with God. Christians' entirely-too-common religion-bashing comments told how the beliefs and actions of religions differ from their own. I spent an entire worship service listening to a non-denominational church denomination–bash my denomination. I was afraid to fill out the visitor's card and tell them the name of my church.

When I love people and resist debating, emotion eventually enters our conversations. There is a point at which the conversation turns toward what we moderns would call the heart of God. This often happens when I ask what people want from their god. Interestingly, most of these answers are similar. The answers (frequently accompanied by tears) include words like *love, acceptance, absolution, wisdom,* and *relief.*

Some people expressed love for God and described a close personal relationship with Him. Usually these people had been through traumatic events that had catapulted them into growth. With tears glistening, one woman said, "I would not have survived without God in my life." Another, "Now I truly understand the peace that passes all understanding." I heard, "I thought I couldn't bear it. Loving God makes the unbearable bearable." Many told me, "Jesus is my closest friend. He and I talk all day." The sweetest answer I heard was, "It was worth all of the pain. It led me back to a relationship with God that I wouldn't trade for anything." These people have discovered the secrets of the *Sh'ma.*

God loves us and tells us so repeatedly in the Bible. Step One to filling our pockets with that love is making an intellectual decision to follow God wherever He leads, mind to Mind. The next five chapters are poignant tales of hope, betrayal, and love that give us a glimpse of how people are following God into incredible places. As we follow Him, mind to Mind, our intellectual love grows deeper each day as we exercise our minds, study the words of God, and learn more about life, love, and God Himself.

CHAPTER 1

If God Opens a Window, Duck!

Then said Jesus to those Jews which believed on him, "If ye continue in my word, then are ye my disciples indeed; And ye shall know the truth, and the truth shall make you free."

(John 8:31-32 KJV)

Holding hands, a couple strolled down by Lake Michigan, their tanned faces lined by a life of hard work. Farmers from Georgia, they found themselves in Wisconsin, living in their camper and helping plant a new church. Their retirement years are devoted to going wherever Christ sends them. The husband's face lit up as he told a story of leading a medical technician to Christ. "God blessed our farming, so we could afford to continue serving Him in retirement."

A friendly waitress in Williams, Arizona, insisted, "Tomorrow is Sunday. You must come to my church. Our pastor is wonderful." Her enthusiasm convinced me, so early the next morning I arrived at First Baptist Church in Williams, Arizona, just in time for a Sunday School class filled with laughter and Bible Study. I was briefly disappointed when I heard their pastor was out of town, but their youth pastor skillfully led us in worship. When they invited me to their covered-dish luncheon, I cheerfully accepted. At that lunch, I got to know Edith Pouquette.

I first noticed Edith during the worship when she called children to the front of the church and held them spellbound with her Bible story. A senior citizen, Edith discovered she had a latent talent for telling stories. Now, she makes the Bible come to life for children through her storytelling. She fills what she had expected to be her retirement days with perparing her stories. "I love what I do. I had to get over my fear of speaking in public, but it was worth it to follow Christ."

Business executives told of risking customers and employment to tell people about Christ. Parents told of leaving high-salaried jobs to have more time with children. Scores of people told of their faithful service to church, community, and family. Business owners told how God had led them into their field. A hotel in Townsend, North Carolina, had Bible verses in their lobby. When I asked about them, the owner told me about Jesus. When I told him about my ministry, he gave me a free night's stay.

God has surprised and blessed these people by their call to discipleship. To them, discipleship meant following God into the unknown, accepting the hardship, and receiving the blessings. None would make any other decision.

You have probably heard the expression, "When God closes a door, He opens a window." Maugie Pastor says, "When God opens this window, you had better duck!" That was certainly true for me. He closed the door of my corporate life and opened a door in ministry. I am still ducking.

I met Maugie while passing through Lafayette, Louisiana. Driving up, I saw a beautiful white gazebo that led to the large white front porch of Aaah! T' Frere's Bed and Breakfast. Ivory lace curtains framed the windows where a large canopy bed enveloped me. Delicious smells of coffee set to brew in the room awakened me. I dressed in front of an ornate French Provincial dresser. Strolling through a colorful garden, I stopped to pet a fluffy cat and entered the house. Smells wafting through the living room led to the incredible Oooo La La Breakfast. Maugie's bright red silk pajamas held the attention of all as her Louisiana drawl directed us to our seats. Mouths watered as we looked at the colorful array of fruits, muffins, and egg soufflé.

I noticed the prayer at breakfast. It was Sunday, and Maugie gave suggestions for worship. "Are you a Christian?" I asked.

Her tinkling laugh lit up the whole room. "Honey, let me tell you my story," she said as she enthusiastically dragged me to her living room. "I'll give you a tour as I talk. We haven't always owned a bed and breakfast. God is full of surprises. Years ago, we were owners of one of Lafayette's most prestigious Cajun restaurants. I was active in the business community and well thought of. Let me tell you, I took pride in my success."

"Suddenly, the economy in Lafayette collapsed. Small businesses closed everywhere. The community couldn't support my elite restaurant. We thought the economy would turn around, so my husband, Pat, and I put all our money into saving our business. We even sold our home."

"I begged God to save our restaurant. I believed He would, but things continued to get worse. Finally, the money ran out. Defeated and discouraged, we gave up. As a public figure, I was embarrassed." She paused to wipe the tears from her eyes.

"I wondered what God was doing. Our family was devastated emotionally and physically. We turned to God and our church. Spiritually, this brought our family closer. In losing everything, we realized what was important."

They still had two of their eight children living at home and had to support them. "Eight children!" I exclaimed. "You must really like children."

Maugie laughed aloud and waved her hands. "I'm Catholic. That's what we do." She continued. "Our church and faith saw us through this transition. God gave me a scripture from Jeremiah. God had plans to prosper me."

"Do you remember the scripture reference?" I asked.

"I told you I was Catholic. We don't memorize things like that."

I joked back, "I'm Baptist, and we want to know things like that." When I went to my room, I did a computer search. Her scripture was Jeremiah 29:11:

"For I know the plans I have for you," declares the LORD, "plans to prosper you and not to harm you, plans to give you hope and a future."

(Jer. 29:11 NIV)

For a time they worked for other people. Being frugal, their financial situation began improving, but they were restless. "God didn't want us too comfortable because He had other plans for us." Pat and Maugie longed to work together again. The last straw was Maugie unfairly losing her restaurant job due to nepotism. "We hit bottom emotionally. We knew we had to go even deeper in our walk with God and fell to our knees. God spoke through a miraculous series of events where His will became clear. We heard Him saying He wanted us to work together and to work for ourselves. We decided to trust God and act.

"By this time, we had saved a little money. We did some calculations. With a small loan, we could buy a small restaurant and start over with a simpler business model. Restaurant work was all we knew. This was our plan. God had other plans."

Pat and Maugie began driving around, dreaming and looking at property. "On one of those drives, we found ourselves looking at a combination gas station and restaurant. I took one look at it and laughed. I may be an excellent decorator, but even I couldn't fix that place. Besides, with all of the fire and oil I use to cook, I would probably ignite the gas in the gas station. We realized we were on the same street as T'Frere's Bed and Breakfast. It had been in our community for years. The current owners had put it up for sale two years ago. We wondered about its fate."

They drove by and saw that it was still for sale. They noticed the real estate agent was a close friend. "I was not interested in buying T'Frere's but seeing my friend's name made me realize that I needed a realtor to help us buy a restaurant. I called her and told her what we were looking for."

"Maugie, you must see this T'Frere's. I can't believe I didn't think of you. It's perfect."

"You're not listening to me," Maugie gently chided. "I said we were looking for a restaurant. I don't want to buy T'Frere's."

"Maugie, you must see this place! It's you. Please take a look," her friend pleaded.

"The minute I went inside, I began visualizing where the art from my former restaurant would go. The house fit my style of furniture perfectly. I fell in love with the place and began mentally decorating it."

Between the two of them, Pat is the accountant. He put pencil to paper. "The place can't make money with the number of bedrooms it currently has." Disappointed, Maugie thought that was the end, but Pat continued figuring. He came back and said, "If we added some additional rooms and kept them booked, it could make money." He investigated Small Business Administration loans and the cost of adding additional rooms.

"By his calculations, the Small Business Administration would lend us enough to build what we needed. We had very little cash, but Pat believed we could scrape together enough to make a 10% down payment. We prayed and God told us to make an offer. The owners accepted within twenty-four hours and left our heads spinning. We made this offer before we had money to purchase it or to redecorate it. We started the paperwork for the loan. We found contractors and began learning about running a bed and breakfast."

If Pat is the accountant, Maugie is the salesperson and marketing specialist. She was concerned about the current customers of T'Frere's. "The owners had given us a key to come with the architect and put a loan package together. When we arrived, I realized they had moved out. I knew that occupancy was the key to success, and I was frantic. The business needed to keep running while the paperwork went through. I called to ask the owners if I could put in an answering machine, check the messages, and book the rooms for them. The owner laughed and suggested we go ahead and move in.

"I went home and told my family to pack, that we were moving in tonight. They thought I had lost my mind. I argued while I packed. God was guiding my steps, and I was afraid to disobey. We moved in with no paperwork signed and no loan in place. We did not have enough rooms to support a business. I began running a business that was owned by others."

This all took place years ago. They got their loan and added the additional rooms. Maugie's eye for decorating created something beautiful. They marketed well and the *Times of Acadiano* reader's poll voted them "Best of the Best." Pat's calculations and business management proved accurate. Maugie's sales and marketing efforts along with her excellent cooking have paid off. They have maintained a 70% occupancy rate since they opened and are financially successful. They paid off the loan with significant returns on their investment.

"Are you happy?" I asked.

She laughed and waved her arms around the room we were standing in. "Look at this. I had better be happy. This was God's plan for my life. He did it all. I am afraid to be anything but happy. This was God's gift to me, and I had better appreciate it."

"May I write your story?" I asked.

"Of course!" she replied. "I tell everyone my story. That's my assignment from God."

CHAPTER 2

If I Only Had a Brain

To the man who pleases him, God gives wisdom, knowledge and happiness, but to the sinner he gives the task of gathering and storing up wealth to hand it over to the one who pleases God. This too is meaningless, a chasing after the wind.

(Eccles. 2:26 NIV)

Have you ever dreamed of being able to "unravel riddles" or understand things like "why the ocean is near the shore"? Do you wish you felt like "dancing and being merry"? Would you like to have the impact of someone like Abraham Lincoln? Perhaps you want to sing a duet of "If I Only Had a Brain" with the Scarecrow from *Wizard of Oz*.

Poor Scarecrow. He was Dorothy's source of wisdom. He helped save a community from a wicked witch. He danced and sang throughout his journey to Oz. Why did he spend the entire time, crying, "If I only had a brain?"

Like the Scarecrow in the *Wizard of Oz*, America is full of educated successful people desperately seeking more worldly knowledge. I know this because I met them as I traveled. Christians and non-Christians were seeking something that was both promising and elusive: knowledge. While easy to acquire, by itself it is never enough.

11

We live in an age where we can have almost any book in the world delivered to our doorstep overnight. The World Wide Web offers unlimited information, and yet Americans continue to seek. With so much knowledge available, why are people still seeking knowledge? If gaining knowledge is the answer to happiness, why are antidepressants the number-one prescription drug sold in America? Perhaps, like the Scarecrow, Americans are crying, "If I only had a brain."

Take for example, Jim and Kim. Unmarried but camping and living together, they were seeking a perfect place to live. They had graduated from college, only to find their newly acquired education was like "chasing after the wind." Much to the dismay of their parents, they went off in search of their *nirvana*. They had tried several different states, but had not located it. I offered my e-mail address and promised to publish the location of *nirvana* on my website if they ever find it.

Both young people had teaching degrees, courtesy of their parents. They were working odd jobs to support their search for happiness. "We have lost faith in educational institutions," they smugly announced. Did their parents wish they had lost faith before so much of their money went to the "unworthy" educational institutions?

"I think we may have to move to another country. We have heard that Australia is a good place to live."

Regretting popping their hopeful balloon, I commented, "I have been there. The cars are a little older, but the people seemed about the same as any place I've been."

"What about God?" I asked. "It sounds like you are looking for a Garden of Eden. Have you thought to ask Him where your Garden of Eden is? The last I heard, God had kicked us out."

"We are spiritual but not religious. All four of our parents came from different religious backgrounds. They couldn't make a decision, so they didn't take us anywhere. We believe that has allowed us to be free from the chains of religion."

I had heard their supposedly unique position many times. Remembering how badly I debate, I resisted the urge. Instead, I challenged, "How do you know you are not religious if you have never tried it? Before you give up on America, why don't you try a Christian church for six weeks? It doesn't much matter what denomination you choose as long as the church believes the Bible and in God the Father, Son, and Holy Ghost. You have nothing to lose. Go every Sunday. Ask your spiritual God to reveal whether Christianity has anything to offer. You just might find what you are seeking. It will be cheaper than plane tickets to Australia, and your parents will be a lot happier. You may even find a use for that education."

Intrigued, Jim and Kim left.

Knowledge is both an essential step on our way to love and the result of the love itself. True knowledge (like wisdom and understanding) comes from God (Proverbs 2:6). To know God is to have an intimate experiential knowledge of Him. Knowledge of God is essential to knowing and fulfilling our calling or purpose in life. The good news is that God will grant us knowledge if we ask for it (2 Chronicles 1:11-12). The bad news is that it does not come from books, the World Wide Web, or moving to another country.

So why are we still seeking knowledge? If we believe what seekers tell us, people continue to seek knowledge to ease constant restlessness that manifests itself in low self-esteem, the constant need for more, or a general dissatisfaction with life. When we accept Christ and follow Him, God gives us the secrets of the kingdom of heaven (Matthew 13:11).

Can you keep a secret? Christians can be like the Scarecrow. Everything we need is available, but many continue crying, "If I only had a brain." The key is found in 2 Peter 1:5-8. When we forget these things, we are "blind and cannot see far away and have forgotten we are purged from our sins."

And beside this, giving all diligence, add to your faith virtue; and to virtue knowledge; And to knowledge temperance; and to temperance patience; and to patience godliness; And to godliness brotherly kindness; and to brotherly kindness charity. For if these things be in you, and abound, they make you that ye shall neither be barren nor unfruitful in the knowledge of our Lord Jesus Christ. But he that lacketh these things is blind, and cannot see afar off, and hath forgotten that he was purged from his old sins.

(2 Pet. 1:5-9 KJV)

CHAPTER 3

Who Needs a Pocket Full of Quarters?

Study to shew thyself approved unto God, a workman that needeth not to be ashamed, rightly dividing the word of truth.

(2 Tim. 2:15 KJV)

Don't you just love having a pocket full of quarters? They are fun, useful, and even essential. We need them for parking meters, vending machines, and phone calls. We have fun using them to play video games. We delight our children by giving them away for candy machines and small rides. Even gumball machines now need a quarter. Quarters make our lives more interesting.

As I traveled across America, I became known as the Pocket Full of Quarters Lady. People loved getting a business card that contained a quarter. For some reason, the metaphor and the term caught on. They remembered Pocket Full of Quarters as both my name and the name of my website. By the end of the journey the quarters were one of the reasons a thousand people per day were going to the website. People seemed to understand that their pockets needed to be full if they were to have an abundant life.

I wish I could take credit for this name, but I cannot. God sent it. In fact, a marketing background caused me to argue with God. At best, the name

Pocket Full of Quarters is abstract and needs explanation. God's ways are mysterious because this turned out to be a catchy name.

When it came time to take the trip—Pocket Full of Quarters—my pockets felt strangely empty. I have a relatively good formal education that includes a bachelor's in music education and a master's in business administration. I have thirty-two additional graduate hours in education and have taken courses in sales, public speaking, and organizational skills. I have taken a large number of Bible Studies, have a few seminary credits under my belt and am a proud graduate of the Seven Habits of Highly Effective People. Why did I feel woefully inadequate when God called me to travel alone across the United States? Steven Covey may have taught me how to "sharpen my sword," but I did not know how to protect myself with one.

Months spent traveling in a black Suburban created the necessity for learning the basics of car maintenance. Camping meant learning about tents, air mattresses, and gas stoves. Seeing the Global Positioning System go into the car meant learning how to use it. I began to grow nervous as strangely shaped, nameless tools entered the car.

In my defense, I have competent men in my life. I began dating my husband when I was sixteen and married him at nineteen. He is the smartest person I know. I have a father, brother, and a husband who can build and/or repair cars, houses, boats, computers, and even airplanes. I have a son who is quickly catching up with the rest of them and comes to my rescue. These men have always taken care of much of the mechanical and physical labor in my life. *God, am I spoiled?*

Learning to Camp

I had never put up a tent. Our friends Bob and Anne were camping mentors and gave wise council. After several trips to camping stores, I asked the teenage sales clerk to help me learn to set up a tent. "It's not that hard, Lady."

"Let's practice anyway," I insisted. By the time I finished putting it up, he fully understood why I wanted to practice. At home, I practiced blowing up air mattresses, setting up a tent, and using Coleman cooking products. I secretly wondered if I would have the nerve to camp alone.

"Can you actually cook?" my daughter asked. I was definitely spoiled.

I set up camp for the first time in Cumberland Falls Camp Ground in Kentucky. By the time the lopsided tent went up, I had drawn a crowd. No one offered to help because watching was too entertaining.

Learning to Change Batteries

My husband had always changed the batteries in our home. Now I find out all of these gadgets have different size batteries, and I have to figure out which one goes in which gadget. I left home with boxes of batteries that I was sure I would never learn to use. I traveled with a refrigerator that was supposed to run off a car battery during the day and a second battery during the night. Unfortunately, it ran the car battery down at night. Now I am an expert at jump-starting my car. I also learned several different technologies before finding one that actually worked with my refrigerator without killing batteries. I can also change all of my own batteries.

Learning New Technology

And what about computer technology? I wrote stories and took pictures while traveling. The plan was to post those stories and pictures on my website as I traveled. Let me set the stage. I was the Chief Executive Officer (CEO) of a computer company. One would think that I knew a little about how to do this. Alas, even in that I was spoiled. CEO's have employees who take care of details for them. This new education constantly vacillated on either side of that fine line between humbling and humiliating.

While on the journey, I had multiple computer problems and even had to replace a computer. I remembered a story told by an elderly woman in a prayer meeting. She believed Satan lived inside her computer, and she performed an exorcism. She reported that her computer started working. Was Satan living in my computer?

Deciding I had nothing to lose, in desperation I laid hands on the computer. Unfortunately, it did not help. What did help was learning about the unmarked check box deep inside Outlook. When I checked the box, I felt like a conquering hero. I remembered a line from Star Trek. "Boldly go where no man (or woman) has gone before."

Learning to Change a Tire

I left town knowing I could not change a tire. I was vaguely uneasy about this vacant spot in my education. While traveling, I even called my mother and said, "You know, I have no idea how to change a tire."

"You could figure it out if you had to," she encouraged. My grandfather owned a service station, so cars are no mystery to her. She was wrong. I should have taken the course, Tires 101.

When I pulled into Hovenweep National Monument in Utah, there were plenty of people there. When I left, I was alone on the mountain. I quickly got into my car and started to pull out. A car pulled up the mountain road and blocked my exit. A lone man sat in the car. My best friend Nancy had predicted duct tape would be involved in my demise. *Does he have duct tape?* I pictured my funeral. Would Nancy say, "I told you so?" Probably. Heart pounding, I grabbed the cell phone. No cell coverage. *OK God, now what?*

"Get out of the car and see what he wants," God said. Or, maybe that was the only choice left to me.

As I got out, the man rolled down his window and asked, "Did you know that your tire is flat?"

No, I did not know. I resisted saying, "Yea, but it is only flat on the bottom." I looked. I guess I needed to confirm his words. Yep. It was flat. I felt a strange combination of emotions. There was relief. *Ax murderers don't begin conversations with politely informing victims of a flat tire.* But what did I know? How many ax murderers had I met? I also felt panic as I realized I could not call AAA. *Is it possible he flattened the tire himself?* Deductive reasoning told me that he would not have flattened my tire, driven down the mountain, and then back up.

I looked at the man who was still in his car with the engine running and said, "I have never changed a tire in my life. I don't even know where the spare or the jack is." I did not tell him that I probably would not recognize a jack. It was over 110 degrees. The man sighed, parked, and got out of the car.

"I'll help you," Ron said. Ron is a single father with joint custody of two children. His ex-wife moved to Seattle with his children, so Ron moved to Seattle to be near them. Currently, he was visiting his mother in the southwest. Ron is a Christian and at one time was active in church. I know all of this because I started asking

18

questions. I can only hope the questioning was a calling from God and not a desire to assure myself that he was not an ax murderer. I did not see any axes.

"Are you going to church in Seattle?" I asked.

"No," he admitted, probably wishing I would stop asking so many questions.

"Well, why not? You are new in town, lonely, and need a church." As I think back over my bossy response, I am not sure why he kept helping me.

"I have been meaning to go to church, but I haven't gotten around to it. You sound like my mother. When I was married, we were active in church. When my marriage fell apart, I lost heart. I need to go back," he confessed.

"If you had found a church by now, God may not have sent you to this mountain to help me. Now you have to listen to me talk about the value of church," I joked.

"I'm sure God sent me up this mountain. It was late, and I was on the way to Mom's. I almost didn't stop." I am sure he resisted the urge to add, "If you knew how to change a tire, God would not have had to send me to you." Feeling unprepared, I prayed a prayer of thanks and wondered what I would have done without Ron.

Ron's first question was, "Where is your jack?"

"What's a jack?" I asked. "JK." At his confusion, I explained that *JK* was short for just kidding. I had been around my college daughter for too long. "At least, I know what a jack is. I wasn't kidding when I said I don't know where it is."

My ego was suffering greatly. I was unprepared. "I'm really not that helpless," I babbled. "I used to run a company."

Ron was kind. "A lot of people don't know how to change a tire." His next question was, "Where is your owner's manual?" At least I knew that answer. I brought it out with pride. Ron warily eyed my heavily packed car. "The jack is under all of that stuff!" We started the laborious process of emptying the car.

Ron got under the car and attached the jack. That was when I noticed him wincing. "I have a bad back from a motorcycle accident," he admitted.

"Move," I ordered. "I'll do the work. You tell me what to do." There is an old saying that if you give a man a fish, you feed him for a meal. If you teach him to fish, you feed him for a lifetime. It was time to learn to change a tire. I prefer that to cleaning a fish.

Ron did the initial setup and put the tire on. From there, he gave directions. I tightened the lugs. Lugs are interesting because they fit either way. Ron was amazingly patient. "You are putting them on backward. Take them off and try again."

I learned about a ratchet. What a marvelous invention. It makes you able to turn things, even if there is not enough room to turn it all the way around.

Finally, we finished changing the tire. "Put the tire in last so you can get it repaired." He handed me the jack. I climbed in the car to fit the jack back into its proper place. That may have been the hardest job of all. I cannot do jigsaw puzzles. After many tries, it finally went in. I thought it positive that I only had one piece left over.

Together, we put all of the equipment back into the car. As we reloaded the impossibly full car, we kept reminding ourselves that everything had come out of this car. We laid the damaged tire on top of the newly created mess. I thanked Ron and left for my destination. Ron went on to hike Hovenweep. I offered him water, diet coke, maps, and food, but he seemed anxious to escape. He did promise to find a church.

Other Educational Opportunities

As I traveled, I learned many things. Did you know that…

- Getting a reclining camp chair to fold up requires training?
- To have electricity at campsites, there is often a switch to turn on?
- It is a good idea to turn off the lantern and shake off bugs before entering a tent?
- Sleeping bags are rated for temperature?
- It gets cold at night in the mountains?
- If you do not fold the tent a certain way, it will not go back into the bag?
- You can get mostly clean without a shower or bathtub?
- There is life after not getting completely clean?
- Bugs do not flavor food?
- It is too windy to camp directly on the shore of Lake Ontario?
- There is a place to put water in an overheated car, other than the radiator cap?

We are God's workmanship, created to do good works (Ephesians 2:10). God actually prepares our work for us in advance and is currently preparing our assignment for next week, month, and year. There is no greater joy than recognizing and acknowledging His preparation.

Our Father needs to have the buildings and roads built in His world. He needs teachers, carpenters, bankers, garbage collectors, and housekeepers. If we want God's approval, we must study and do quality work (2 Timothy 2:15). Training benefits us in this life and the next one (1 Timothy 4:7-8), so we must not be a slouch. This concept has eternal consequences. If we understand that we are on assignment from God, we will find purpose in a job well done and prepare ourselves for our assignments.

The most important thing I learned on my first Pocket Full of Quarters journey was how to depend on God to meet all the needs in my life. Now, if only I am able to apply that knowledge to the rest of my life.

CHAPTER 4

The "Pick One" Strategy

And this is the confidence that we have in him, that, if we ask any thing according to his will, he heareth us.

(1 John 5:14 KJV)

Do you have trouble making decisions? Perhaps decision making seems like too much pressure. Maybe you have too many good choices. Are you terrified of making bad decisions? Relax. This can all change. You can be decisive. A mind that loves God will make wise decisions.

If you have trouble making decisions, perhaps you should try a strategy passed on by one of my Christian mentors. Simply pick an answer and go with it. Could decisions really be this simple? Yes, if you know when to pick one and if you believe the Bible.

"What if I make the wrong decision?" I argued with my mentor.

My mentor laughed at me. "Where is your faith? If you ask for wisdom, God will tell you what to do. Think about the important decisions in your life. When Bob proposed, you knew the answer. You probably know the answer about most of the important stuff. Now think about the decisions you are struggling with." I immediately thought about how much trouble my girlfriend and I have picking a place for lunch. I also remembered the hours my business partners and I spent debating the exact shade of teal for office paint.

He continued. "What people struggle over are usually things that don't really matter. If you have to make a decision, pray. Check it against the Bible. If the answer is directly in the Bible, do what it says. If you still do not know what to do, pick an alternative. Pick an answer that does not conflict with the Bible. Use a dartboard or flip a coin but pick one. It is better to be wrong than to be indecisive. Most of the time, you will pick the right answer."

Since 1979, I have tried to get up every morning and ask God for knowledge of His will and the power to carry it out. It is preposterous to ask and then doubt the answer. When I do not know what to do, I pick an answer. When I remember to read the Bible, pray for wisdom, pick an answer, and to act immediately, God faithfully rewards me.

I applied this strategy to the trip across America. I studied maps. They offered endless directions. I talked to people and gathered information. There were numerous suggestions. I read the Bible. No, it didn't say which highway to take. I prayed for wisdom and applied the pick-one strategy. An adventure that defied human explanation unfolded. It included mountains, storms, oceans, geysers, amusement parks, and art galleries.

I love art galleries. I thrill at seeing the work of great artists. There is delight to be found in wandering through small private galleries. One can see a clear difference in the vibrant colors and detailed brush strokes of talented artists. It is fascinating to see the differences in how artists capture light. There are elements of imagination unique to each artist.

I am particularly fond of artists who paint from memory and fill in the gaps with creativity. Because I like oceans, seascapes always get my attention. For some, painting is a relaxing hobby. For a select few, it is doing what God created them to do.

While traveling, I visited my friend Kimberly in Carmel. Kimberly is one of our brave heroes in the military. She and I spent a wonderful day going to church and enjoying the spectacular beauty of God's creations in California. We tiptoed barefoot around seaweed on a beach and laughed at seals frolicking in the water.

While strolling through Carmel, California, a sign saying Roger Budney Fine Art caught my eye. I felt the Spirit of God urging me to enter. Apologetically, I looked at Kimberly and asked if she minded. A good sport, Kimberly went in with me, prepared for what she knew might be a long visit.

I was lost in reverence as I stared at the work. Various colors of a wind-swept ocean leapt off the canvas. I wondered about the fate of the small wind-tossed boats. Swirling clouds threatened doom for all caught in their wake. I jumped when someone said, "May I help you?"

"Tell me about the artist that painted this picture," I whispered.

The man smiled. "I am the artist. My name is Roger Budney."

I introduced myself and quickly explained that I was only looking. "I won't be making large purchases anytime soon," I apologized. "Your work is beautiful."

"Where are you from?" he asked.

"Jacksonville," I said and filled in the details.

He smiled. "I know Jacksonville well. I used to sell insurance there."

I gasped. "You must have hated selling insurance if you can paint like this," I blurted out.

"Actually, you are right. I have always loved to paint. I tried to paint as a hobby because I had seen too many starving artists. I didn't believe I could support a family by painting. The entire time I sold insurance, I was restless. My wife prayed for me constantly. I was committed to the insurance field and made money, but I was never happy. We moved to California. I stayed in insurance for a while but continued to feel restless. I put a few of my paintings in a gallery, and they sold quickly. I was delighted and surprised. I longed to do this full time."

Roger and his wife, Barbara, are Christians. They sought God's leadership before making any decisions. "We searched the Bible, but it didn't give us a direct answer. It did talk about fulfilling God's purpose for my life and trusting God. We talked to our minister. We prayed and made a decision to trust God with my talent.

"My first step was to open a smaller shared gallery in another part of town. I did reasonably well. Then I felt God saying, "Go further." I found a partner and moved into this area. The rent is more, but the local community and tourists support this area. We were worried about making the financial commitment, but again we prayed and made the decision. We took a deep breath and gave a deposit on this place."

"How is it doing?" I asked.

He smiled. "One of the blessings and the difficulties of prayer is that God answers it. I am now a businessman, a marketing department, and an artist. My restlessness is gone. I have traded restlessness for cash flow and profit issues."

"Is it worth it?"

"Oh, yes. I make less money but that gets better every day. Painting is what I was created to do."

We can make bold decisions because Christians do not stand alone (John 8:16-17). Like Jesus, we stand with the Father and can trust our decisions. Like Roger Budney, we can use the mind God gave us and be decisive.

CHAPTER 5

Held Hostage

Set your mind on the things above, not on the things that are on earth.

(Colossians 3:2 NASB)

Is it possible to take our thoughts captive in a nation that constantly bombards us with ungodly pictures, words, and choices? Watching murder and mayhem on the news feeds our fears. Watching beautiful and successful people feeds our insecurities, greed, and vanity. Is it any wonder that our wandering thoughts travel roads of terror, insecurity, grandiosity, or fury?

When you spend four months alone on the road, you can imagine all sorts of things. Are people following you? Is your car making a new noise? Is that a bear, an ax murderer, or a cat outside your tent? These wayward thoughts interfere with the ability to hear the voice of God. Part of loving God with our minds includes making our wayward minds behave. We are to exercise self-control regarding our thoughts.

The first Pocket Full of Quarters journey was a calling from God. I felt a sense of reverence about it. I wanted to be worthy. I knew that it was God's job to make me holy. As I prepared for the journey, I wondered about my role in being holy.

One of my mentors suggested that I needed to study sanctification. I only had a vague sense of what that really meant. I began my research.

I discovered that it was God's job to sanctify me. My morning Bible study included 1 Thessalonians 5:23-24 where Paul had actually prayed for my sanctification. I began praying his prayer. "Father, God of peace. I ask you to sanctify me, through and through. May my whole spirit, soul, and body be kept blameless." I read God's promise that He would call me faithful and answer my prayer.

I read further and found John 17:15-19. Imagine—Jesus had gone to the Father on my behalf. I was overwhelmed that Jesus prayed for me. How could I lose? I would be traveling and meeting people. Jesus had sent me on this journey. The Scriptures say He wants me to be *in* the world but not *of* the world. He asked the Father to sanctify me by truth. He sanctified Himself, so that I could be truly sanctified. How blessed I felt.

I knew truth was in the Scriptures. I searched them. I found that I was supposed to test everything and to hold on to the good. 1 Thessalonians 5:21-22 says to avoid every kind of evil. I had my instructions.

"Now wait a minute," I thought. "Surely, this scripture did not mean every kind of evil." Some sins seemed so small that I did not think they really mattered. After all, I would be passing lots of casinos. We do not have casinos in North Florida. Really, how could one small quarter hurt? I needed a definition for evil. I love jewelry. When I was employed, buying jewelry was a fun pastime. Now I was unemployed. Did that make buying jewelry evil? Perhaps, I was going too far, I rationalized. *But God*, I argued. *People stop me to talk about my jewelry. It leads to conversations about you. So, new jewelry is important.* Was that God laughing?

God, an occasional quarter probably does not make a difference. Drivers are going to cut me off. How can I keep from being angry? Hotels are noisy, and maids will knock on my door too early. You know that when I'm tired, I can be grumpy. No one can blame me for that. You made me that way. I will be passing through interesting places with interesting food. Can't I occasionally splurge? I continued to whine to God.

God was clear. He sent me Psalms 4:3. "I am setting you apart for this trip. I want better from you. Do not worry. You will fail, but you will learn from it. I will help you. You are already forgiven for your slips."

I found 1 Corinthians 2:13. I felt Him saying, "I want you to speak with my words. To do that, you have to be able to hear my voice. I do not want anything between you and me."

In Isaiah 6:1, I heard Him saying, "I have sent you on this trip, and I will go with you."

I went to my knees and asked God to help me. I took my wayward thoughts captive and listened to the voice of God. He gave special instructions for a special time in my life. For purposes of the Pocket Full of Quarters journey, God led me to the following decisions.

Starve the Flesh

- Food: Keep it simple. I ate vegetables, fruit, meat, and an occasional rice cake. I did most of my own cooking. Most meals were fast and simple.
- Distractions: Keep them to a minimum. I avoided TV, secular radio, movies, and newspapers.
- Gambling: Certainly no quarters in slot machines! Not even one.
- Mood Altering Substances: None! Since I do not drink, this was not a problem.
- Attitude: Not to give in to the frustrations that go with the inconveniences of traveling. I was to look for what was right with the world and not what was wrong with the world.

Feed the Spirit

- Corporate Worship: To worship with other believers every Sunday and any other opportunity I was given. I was to visit different Christian denominations.
- Private Worship: To worship at every stop I made.
- Bible Study and Devotions: To begin every morning with devotions and Bible Study. I was already in this habit.
- Pray Without Ceasing: To pray continually, particularly at every stop.
- Christian Music: To listen to and sing Christian music continually while traveling.

- Writing: I wrote the stories of the people I met and the places and churches I visited. I was led to make every story a Bible study.
- To Praise God in All Things: Flat tires, fear, broken equipment, and loneliness included.
- Exercise: To exercise every morning and to hike whenever the opportunity presented itself.
- Witness: To talk to everyone I met. I was to listen to their stories and share the love of Christ with them.
- Help: I was to offer help everywhere.

There has never been a time in my life when I felt so loved as when I was on the first journey of Pocket Full of Quarters. He blessed me with scenic beauty, difficulties, worship, knowledge, understanding, and fun. I went through my days with an energy that I did not believe was possible. I wrote late into the night. I woke refreshed. I felt clean and pure. I could hear God's voice and was amazed at the assignments He sent.

I made friends all over our country. Strangers invited me into their homes. I visited with relatives I had only seen a few times in my life. People poured out their hearts to me. They listened when I talked. I felt God's words in my mouth. Sharing the love of God and the message of Christ came easily because I felt it so strongly.

I returned home with an entirely different attitude about the people around me. I have stayed in contact with many of the people that I met on the trip. I am close to relatives that I barely knew before. I have made new friends in my church as I became curious about the stories in my own backyard. I connect with the people I meet and have many opportunities to share the love of Christ.

While traveling, churches adopted, loved, and taught me. I began to feel a part of every church I visited. I began to understand the concept of one church. I heard God's love everywhere I went. The churches I visited were more alike than they were different. I looked for the good in the churches I visited. Off-key singing became a joyful noise. Different worship styles became an opportunity to learn. I lost the concept of a boring sermon. Now I wonder how anyone talking about the word of God could be boring. I have returned home grateful for my church. There is nowhere I would rather worship.

Deciding to see everything as a blessing has changed me. I see change and problems as opportunities instead of losses. On the trip, a flat tire on a lonely mountain was an opportunity to witness. A near car accident when the truck ahead of me had a blow out introduced me to two delightful young men. Windstorms in a tent became an opportunity for faith. When I returned home, my husband was losing his job. God had a true adventure planned for us.

I drove at least four hours every day. That was a time for worship. I listened, sang, and prayed. I began to understand what worship really meant. Now I listen to Christian music often. Music is playing as I am writing this. I am hearing the words, "We will glorify the Lord of Lords who is the Great I Am." I stopped for a moment to glorify the Lord of Lords.

I was amazed at how much need I saw when I began to look. I found people stranded by the road who needed the tools in my car. I found children lost in malls, and senior citizens lost in parking lots. I offered pillows and blankets to people sleeping on floors in hospitals. Camping equipment could aid others in campgrounds. Material possessions became tools for my calling. I began to understand that everything belongs to God for Him to use in His service.

I see the world differently. Everything is an adventure when I have a heavenly perspective. When earthly thoughts threaten to overwhelm me, I stomp my foot. I am on my way to heaven. I don't want earthly thoughts holding me hostage.

STEP TWO

Please God, heart to Heart

And thou shalt love the Lord thy God with all thy heart.

(Mark 12:30 KJV)

How would others say you react when angry, surprised, or disappointed? If you hear words like *powder keg*, *hot tempered*, *distant*, *hard*, or *emotional*, it does not bode well for your emotional maturity level. In the first section, we saw examples of people loving God with their minds. Step 2 in the process of loving God is to engage our emotions in this never-ending adventure of seeking to be one with our Creator. This section is devoted to the emotional maturity needed to love God, our heart to His Heart.

In ancient times, Hebrews thought emotions came from the bowels. Today, we refer to the heart when referring to our emotions. A grade-school teacher described herself as tenderhearted while she was explaining why she could not keep order in a troubled classroom. A woman described her husband as hardhearted. The description of his behavior sounded mean.

When we pray for God to soften a heart, we are usually pleading with God to give a loved one understanding. The common expression, "It almost gave me a heart attack," means a circumstance deeply disturbed us. For us, heart and emotions go hand in hand. For purposes of this section, I will be using the modern interpretation of the heart as the center of our emotions.

While traveling, I learned to watch emotions to gauge the responsiveness of people. One observation was that the condition of their hearts seemed to run parallel to the description of their relationship with God. For example, a woman who said she had lost faith in God had also lost faith in herself, others, and her life. Alcoholism, abuse, and the eventual death of her spouse had broken her already fragile heart.

I met a woman who basked in the glory of God's grace. Not only had God forgiven her, she had forgiven herself for tragic past mistakes that caused the death of her child. The Bible says that what we say is a mirror of our hearts. I have found that people usually reveal the condition of the heart in the first five minutes of conversation.

I also began to watch emotions to gauge the responsiveness of churches. When I entered The Church At Cross Gate Center of Hot Springs, Arkansas, it was obvious they had heart. A smiling greeter firmly clasped my hand and escorted me to Thelma, my heartwarming hostess for the service. Within five minutes, Thelma communicated her love for her church, husband, children, grandchildren, and me. The Church at Cross Gate Center worshippers responded eagerly to all aspects of the service. They sang and clapped with all of their heart. Their heartfelt love for their pastor showed as they eagerly took sermon notes and gave hearty Amens.

Marsh Corner Community Church in Methuen, Massachusetts, has a heart for leading people to Christ. I almost didn't go to church that morning. I had left Maine the day before and could not find a hotel. I had to drive all the way to Massachusetts. I arrived late and knew I would be tired the next morning.

I asked the hotel staff about churches.

"We don't have any," the tired desk clerk announced.

"I promise, you have churches in your area." I told him a little about Pocket Full of Quarters and my testimony.

Though I hadn't missed a single Sunday on the journey, I called my husband and confessed that I might miss the next morning. After all, it was after midnight, and I had no ideas for where to worship. Surely God understood.

As I talked to Bob, I realized that I was really asking for permission. When we hung up, I looked in the Yellow Pages and picked a church that was near an exit that I had just passed.

Tired as I was, I felt God's presence as soon as I walked into the building. The worship was a wonderful blend of singing, Bible reading, sermon, and the Lord's Supper. As I listened to their pastor, Rev. Stephen Jeans, I was impressed with his leadership skills. He spoke clearly about what was important in this church. He firmly stated that they serve a God of love. I watched people laughing and hugging as they lingered outside the building. It was as if they didn't want to leave each other.

Church members Ron and Dottie Beldon invited me to lunch. Active in church, Ron led the music in the early service, and Dottie helped with the women's ministry. I first noticed Ron and Dottie because they sat in church with their arms around each other.

Ron and Dottie took me to a delightful place right on the water. Our table was outside. After we prayed and ate together we had fun feeding the ducks, geese, and fish as Ron and Dottie shared their testimony.

They were not Christians when they married and began their family. When their children were four and seven, Marsh Corner offered to bus their children to church. Ron confessed, "We liked the idea of a Sunday morning all to ourselves. We felt our children would be safe, and said yes."

The children loved the church and couldn't wait to return each Sunday. One Sunday, their son asked, "Why do we go to church without you?" Ron and Dottie looked at each other and admitted it was a good question. They attended the next Sunday. It took a while, but they finally became Christians. This all took place years ago. Their children are now adults, and their entire family serves Christ in His church.

Mars Hill Fellowship in Seattle, Washington, has a heart for reaching the young. Their service was a normal blend of prayer, Bible reading, singing, sermon, and the Lord's Supper. The blaring guitars, contemporary music, and casually dressed ministers offered a worship style appealing for the young at heart. Their recent Bible School led twenty-seven children to commit their hearts to Jesus Christ.

As I talked to people, visited churches, and studied the Bible, I began to realize that it takes a whole and healthy heart to fully love God. God wants us free from the pain and regrets of our past. His grace allows this. He wants us to feel free to enjoy and express our emotions. He wants us to have a childlike heart that is free to play, laugh, and make a joyful noise. He offers peace no matter the circumstance.

So take heart. Breathe deeply and feel your chest relaxing. Read the stories of people learning to love God with all their hearts.

CHAPTER 6

A Pocket Full of Tears

But I am poor and sorrowful: let thy salvation, O God, set me up on high. I will praise the name of God with a song, and will magnify him with thanksgiving.

(Ps. 69:29-30 KJV)

Have you ever had your heart broken? If the answer is no, you may be tempted to skip this chapter. Please read it anyway. You may need it to fill your pockets to prepare for a bleak future. You can rest assured that your heart will be broken at some time in your life.

Why can I say that with such authority? It is only logical. Think about all of the bad things just lurking around the corner–crime, accidents, war, death, health issues, natural disasters, and divorce. Don't forget about job loss, children failing in school, and spouses being unfaithful. If those do not get us, there is always your favorite football team losing, not getting that raise, and friends stabbing us in the back. Satan knows us well and is on a mission to destroy our hearts. He will use any tools available to him.

In a world where Satan rules, is it any wonder that so many have broken hearts? The Bible says Satan is a prowling lion waiting to devour us. Look at what Satan did to Job. The prowling lion took Job's possessions, health, and family.

Why would God allow such things to happen? I do not know the answer to that, but at least the Bible warns us about what to expect. As I traveled across America, I was reminded repeatedly about the difficulty of living in this world.

We get no choice about having our hearts broken, but we do get a choice about our response. For example, I met a woman who as a child was continuously sexually abused by her father. For her entire life she has sought healing from psychologists. It was the first thing she talked about in our conversation. Her father broke her heart. It's still broken. I suggested a different approach to her healing.

Let us look at a story with a completely different outcome. I met a man who grew up in an orphanage. He lost his entire loving family before the age of eight. It broke his heart. This orphanage was kind and loving and took him to a kind and loving church. He allowed the orphanage and church to become his new family. He allowed God to heal his broken heart. Now he loves God with a healthy and whole heart.

I watched happy eleven-year-old Amanda chasing her cousins at a campsite. As I talked to her aunt, Amanda joined the conversation. She soon realized that I was looking for stories. "I watched Daddy die when I was nine. He fell to the floor and wouldn't wake up. I called 911, but they couldn't help." After giving details of the funeral, she excitedly said, "Mommy is getting married again."

"You seem so happy. Some people never get over what you experienced. What made the difference?"

"God helped me," she said matter-of-factly. "We go to church. Everyone came to our house. The pastor said God would heal my heart, but only if I let Him. I started talking to God, and He made me feel better. Now I will have a new daddy. I'm glad God healed my heart. This way, I can love my first daddy and my second daddy too."

A woman lost her husband on Christmas day. He died early that morning without warning. She had to plan his funeral with his gifts still under the Christmas tree. "My church was wonderful," she said. "My pastor missed Christmas with his family to come to me. Everyone surrounded me with love, love, love. God was so good to me."

"Is Christmas hard for you?" I asked.

"Certainly not," she said. "My husband went to be with Jesus on Christmas. What better Christmas present could he have had? At first I was upset, but I had a dream about him. I saw him in heaven eating an ice cream cone. He was healthy and happy. He had been sick for so long. When I woke, I knew it would be selfish to want him on earth again."

We need a whole and healthy heart to love God with our entire heart. A damaged or dead heart is not whole. Some never get over heartbreaks. Instead, they go through life collecting a pocket full of tears.

I met Mallory when I was trying to buy a hat.

I am not very observant. Two months into the trip, I finally noticed that everyone out West wears hats while hiking. One-hundred-five degrees is hot. I went into a gift shop where Mallory sold me a hat and a ticket for a night cruise down the Colorado River.

Mallory was a college student working a summer job. I noticed her immediately because of her stooped shoulders. Her eyes had the round, dark hollows of someone spending long hours in an ICU waiting room. What terrible things had happened to Mallory? Because it was Saturday night, I asked her about churches for the next day.

"There are no good ones here," she muttered dejectedly, not meeting my eyes.

I laughed. "I guess I know your opinion about churches here." Sheepishly, she went on to make a couple of suggestions. "Do you go to church anywhere?" I asked.

"I'm Catholic, but I don't go. I have gone to an evening Bible Study, but I quit."

"Are you a Christian?" I inquired.

"I was baptized as a baby."

"Most Catholics are. Have you personally decided to make Christ a part of your life?" I pursued.

"Well, I liked the Bible Study," she hedged.

Hmm, I thought. *We need another approach.* "What is your favorite book in the Bible?"

Surprisingly, she had no trouble answering. "Genesis." I was surprised because I usually hear Psalms, Proverbs, or one of the four Gospels. I have even heard Revelation but never Genesis.

"Why?"

She began telling her story. "Grandma was a Christian and a Baptist. She studied the Bible continuously and loved the number seven in Genesis. She also loved stars. Grandma got sick and had an operation. She actually died on the operating table, but they brought her back to life. She was never the same again. She said she had seen a glimpse of heaven and was ready to die. She even stopped eating. I begged her to eat."

"You don't understand," Grandma would say. "It is time for me to die. I am at peace."

Mallory stopped to wipe her eyes. "I gave up the rest of my life and spent every day with her. Eventually, she went to the hospital. As she lay dying, she kept talking about seeing the beautiful bowing and dancing seven stars. She said someone nice was there with her. I believe my grandmother was seeing heaven and the stars mentioned in Genesis. I guess I do believe in heaven and God."

"It sounds like your grandmother had a personal relationship with God. She probably let you see it because she wanted the same thing for you. Do you have any relationship with God?

"No," she admitted. "I've had too many losses in my life. I'd have trouble being close to a God that took so much from me."

"What have you lost?"

"I lost three grandparents. When I was fourteen years old, my boyfriend was killed in an accident. I grew up right here in this city. Fourteen of my friends and classmates died in car accidents while I was in school." As she talked, her crying grew worse. Her losses were years old. Suddenly I understood the stooped shoulders and the hollow eyes.

"I'm sorry," she said, wiping her eyes and sniffing. "I didn't mean to cry."

I breathed a prayer of thanks that we were the only people in the gift shop. I prayed for help. "Do you want this pain to get better?"

"My pain can't go away. These people are not coming back."

"Mallory, I promise you can be free of pain," I said. "I speak from experience. There is an answer." By this time, I was crying too. I shared the losses in my life. I talked about people I had met on the journey. I talked about the lives God had turned around and the hearts He had healed.

"You are collecting pain. You have a pocket full of tears. You have been walking through life, taking each painful experience and adding it to the collection in your pockets. Your pockets are bulging. You need to empty them." I stopped to take a breath. I had not meant to make such an impassioned plea. I hoped I had spoken God's words and not mine.

"What do I do?" she asked. "I've been to the churches here. They don't help people focus on God." I decided not to argue with her. What mattered was that she believed she was right.

"What about where you go to college?" I asked. "Have you tried the churches there?'

"No," she admitted.

"Do you really want me to suggest what to do?" I asked.

"Yes," she murmured.

"OK, I'll make some suggestions. First, settle the issue about Jesus. Ask Him into your life. Tell Him about your pain. Confess your mistakes. Make Him a part of your life. Next, when you get back to college, find a Christian church with a strong college program. Get active. Go to Sunday School and church. Get in a weekly Bible Study. Begin doing morning devotions and never miss a day. Tell God what is hurting you. Give Him your pain. Ask Him what you should do with your life. Fill your pockets with God, so you have no room for tears. I promise you things will get better."

As I left, I prayed for Mallory. I asked others to pray for her. I felt a brief moment of panic. I had made big promises and knew many unhappy Christians. Had I mis-spoken? No, I decided. God is faithful. *Oh God, you are faithful. Forgive my doubt. If she seeks you, please be there for her.*

With most people, I never found out the rest of the story. The next summer I journeyed back to the same spot, wondering if Mallory would be working there again. When I arrived at the gift shop, I saw someone who favored Mallory. Could this possibly be her? This young woman was standing tall, animated, and laughing. Her eyes were alive. "Did you work here last summer?" I tentatively asked.

"Yes," she gasped. "You're the Pocket Full of Quarters lady. I did everything you suggested. It worked. I'm happy. People must tell you all the time how much you helped them."

I laughed. "No, not really. Sometimes they tell me to mind my own business. Mostly, I never know the end of the story."

The gift shop was busy. She took the next customer. I left crying. God is faithful. Why was I surprised and amazed? *Thank you Father. Forgive my lack of faith.*

CHAPTER 7

False Evidence Appearing Real

He shall not be afraid of evil tidings: his heart is fixed, trusting in the LORD.

(Ps. 112:7 KJV)

*H*ave you ever heard a pack of barking coyotes? Fear is waking up and hearing them surrounding your tent. Fear is driving through five New England states at night in blinding rain and finding "no room at the inn." Riding a subway alone at night in downtown Chicago and feeling sudden confusion about the next stop will get your attention. Then there was sleeping on Lake Ontario in wind so strong that it actually lifted the mattress. In each case, my heart hammered as adrenaline surged. Senses heightened in preparation for impending disaster. I was prepared for fight or flight.

Fear can be both lifesaving and deadly. Reacting inappropriately can cause the very thing we worry about. Panic on the subway tempted me to get off at the wrong stop. Fear of wind almost made me pack up in the middle of the night to drive exhausted through a storm in unfamiliar territory. Fear prepares us for action. Asking for God's wisdom allows sound reactions.

When I was twelve years old, I was happily tromping through the lush green woods of Georgia with thirteen-year-old Andy. Suddenly he screamed, "Stop. Do not move!" I looked down to see a rattlesnake six inches from my foot and poised to strike. I froze. The snake and I stared at each other. "I'll be back. Do not move," Andy cried.

I stood rooted to the spot with a feeling that I was living in a nightmare. It seemed like hours until he returned, though it was only minutes. The snake remained coiled and ready. My shorts and sneakers offered little protection.

Andy returned, stopped a safe distance away, confidently raised a gun to his shoulder, and blew the head off the snake.

At that instant, he became my first love.

You are probably shocked. *Children playing with guns?* OK, you are right. The possible outcomes of my afternoon are frightening. That is not the point of the story. Besides, Andy grew up in the country. Times were different. He knew how to use guns for protection and food. He was an accurate shot, and I knew it. He used his gun with his family's permission and never abused the privilege. It did not occur to either of us that he would miss.

Some say F.E.A.R. is an acronym for "False Evidence Appearing Real"—an interesting acronym that often applies. In other circumstances, a gun would have been something to fear. Standing within striking distance of a rattlesnake, fear of the gun could have caused me to flinch and be bitten. Andy and the gun were the rescuers. The snake was the enemy.

A heart that loves God knows how to distinguish between healthy fear and false evidence appearing real. It can separate dread from fear and find the courage to take the bold steps required of a disciple of Christ. 1 Peter 3:6 says to do what is right and not give way to fear! When fear knocks at our door, we say *No, thank you*, and slam the door. We rebuke it. We do not give it a foothold. We turn our backs on it. We obey God and do what is right.

When our knees knock with fear we can turn to Isaiah 35:3-4 and pray, "Dear God, strengthen our weak hands and steady our knocking knees." We all feel fear. Our response to fear is the difference between courage and cowardice. Have you ever heard the expression, "Courage is fear that has said its prayers"? The secret to driving out fear is perfect love (1 John 4:18). There is no fear in love. A heart that loves God drives out fear.

Driving Pike's Peak causes fear for many. I stopped at a tourist information center to ask for directions. Smiling at me was a man with a wrinkled, weathered face deeply etched with years of laughter. He cheerfully gave me directions and offered me driving tips.

"Is driving Pike's Peak really worth it?" I asked.

"I like it." He got a devilish gleam in his eye. "But I like you, too. You tell me how good my judgment is." God forgive me, but it still flatters me to be flirted with. Maybe I will write about the sin of pride in my next book. I smiled.

Somehow, Uncle Bobby and Aunt Catherine managed to always keep up with where I was. My Aunt Catherine constantly worried about my being caught in a flash flood out West. Uncle Bobby had the uncanny ability to anticipate my actions. He called with a dire warning. "Do not drive Pike's Peak. It's too steep. Your brakes will burn out."

Daddy called. "Don't you dare drive Pike's Peak. Take the train or bus." Honest, I planned to take their advice. When I arrived at Pike's Peak, the buses and trains were full. I talked to the park attendant about the safety of driving. He had a quiz prepared for the uninitiated:

"How much mountain driving have you done?" I reported teaching school in the Allegany Mountains and driving from school to school. I mentioned my driving across America.

"What's different about driving mountain roads?" he asked.

I replied, "You use gears instead of brakes. It helps to turn the air conditioner off on the way up and to turn it on going down. Watching gauges is also important."

"What kind of car are you driving?" The black Suburban was acceptable.

"How are your tires?" They were new.

"Ma'am, you will be fine. Have fun and be careful." Visions of Daddy's brakes overheating near Ruby Falls taunted me. I decided my fear was false evidence appearing real. It was a steep drive, but I felt prepared.

At first, it wasn't too bad. The paved road wound gently up the densely forested mountain road. It got steeper as my car traveled past cliffs offering views of green rolling hills. Suddenly, I did not know it was possible for a road to be so steep. Dust flew everywhere from the now dirt-and-gravel road. Surely, the car was going to slide back down the hill. Multitasking would not work here. I turned my cell phone off. I pulled over when it was time to change the CD player playing the much needed worship music.

I watched gauges. They were normal. *What if they are broken?* False evidence was appearing real. I turned on my headlights. I kept both hands on the wheel. I made the mistake of looking left and gulped. No rails and an endless drop. *How was I going to get back down?* I stopped to enjoy the cool air and breathtaking expanse of God's creation. An emerald green lake far below seemed to be waiting for my car to take the plunge.

As a child, I used to ride with my grandfather on dirt roads. We talked about stopping and taking turns. "When you stop on dirt roads, you have to use a lighter brake. Find the speed your car rides the smoothest. You have more control going a little faster." I was never too sure how much control he actually had, but I always knew he was having fun.

I have a confession about my driving. I tend to drive in the direction that I look. Did I mention there were no rails? Now, I was above the tree line. It is good to know one's limitations. If I liked a view, I stopped to enjoy it.

Along the road, I passed terrified people, clutching the steering wheel. They were creeping along the gravel road, shaking themselves to death with the bumps. "Go faster," I felt my grandfather whisper." I sped up, and my car stopped bumping. I realized I was enjoying myself. God had removed the fear and replaced it with exhilaration.

When I got to the top, I felt like a conquering hero. I went to the overlooks and worshiped God as I stared at his marvelous universe. A giant eagle swooped below. I felt so blessed. *Thank you for leading me to this experience. Help me to drive back down safely.*

Signs warned: Do Not Use Brakes. Hot Brakes Can Fail!

Unfortunately, no brakes meant faster driving. Terror tempted drivers to slow down. Ironically, the faster speed was safer.

I got behind a woman traveling at five miles per hour. She never took her foot off the brake. She did not pull over to let people around her. Her fear was endangering both of us. *Am I really going to have to pass on this road?* I waited for a wider area. Passing on a narrow steep road was frightening, but I recognized the false evidence being presented to me. I closed my eyes and went around. Just kidding. I carefully passed her with open eyes.

As I passed this woman, I thought about her fear. Her goal was to avoid going over the cliffs. If she burned out her brakes, she would have caused her fear to come true. I sped up so that if her brakes burned up, I would be well out of her way. Fortunately, for this woman, park rangers were looking out for her. There was a halfway point to check brake temperature. One too many had gone over those cliffs.

My brake temperature was fine. Driving through the checkpoint, I smugly glanced at the cars pulled off the road. Was that pride I was feeling? I have to work on that. The uniformed attendant sternly warned, "Use low gear and not your brakes!" I resisted the urge to salute as I said, "Yes sir!"

You might wonder why I would take such a steep drive. It is simple. God led me there. Besides, I wanted to reap the rewards. The view was beautiful. I loved it. Later, I talked to a family who had made that challenging trip. The stern man at the checkpoint stopped them. "I will never do it again," the father reported. "It was too dangerous." If he drove like the woman I briefly trailed, I have to agree. It was too dangerous to be driving Pike's Peak while riding your brakes. For me, it was worth it.

CHAPTER 8

Why, Daddy, Why?

Understanding is a wellspring of life unto him that hath it.

(Prov. 16:22 KJV)

Years ago, we lived in a remote wooded area circling a golf course. The circle, combined with a lack of stop signs, encouraged "hot-rodders." The remoteness gave a false sense of security about the safety of the street. Sadly, our family sacrificed a dog and a cat at the altar of foolish drivers. One day, our beautiful seven-year-old sable-and-white Sheltie, Daisy, spotted a horse and rider. Her herding instincts took over. Before we could react, she bolted after the horse and into a path of a speeding car.

When our new kitten darted out of the house and was crushed by a careening car, my young son, Chris, dryly stated, "I wonder how long we'll have Kelley."

What did Chris mean? He knew his beloved pets were dead, and he understood why. He also understood the threat of the deadly road to his little sister, Kelley. Chris's question helped me understand that no matter how much I tried to protect my loved ones, that road presented more risk than I was willing to take. The For Sale sign went up the next week.

As soon as our little prodigies can talk, they begin plaguing us with the word why. Why is the sky blue? Why do I have to go to bed? Why do birds sing?

Why, why, why? Do the questions stop when we reach adulthood? You know the answer. Why do my thighs bulge in my jeans? Why did my child have to get sick and die? Why is cancer eating my body? Like little children, we badger our Father with our perpetual God-given need for understanding.

I visited the Fountain of Angels at the Precious Moments Chapel in Carthage, Missouri. The water and lights danced with vivid changing color as the angels told the story of creation. Suddenly, Jesus' face appeared out of the darkness. I watched the crowd. As understanding dawned, tears began to flow. I tried to comfort the woman behind me. "I didn't understand creation before seeing this," she sobbed. Creation is meaningless without a Creator. Proverbs 16:22 says understanding is our fountain of life.

The Pocket Full of Quarters journey led through many hiking trails. Being a wimpy hiker, I carefully checked the length and conditions of possible trails. Five miles over moderate elevations is a stretch. One afternoon, I made a wrong turn in 105-degree weather. The hiking time and distance suddenly doubled. The wrong path led through steeper and rougher trails. My water supply was insufficient for my comfort. I finally arrived at the car exhausted and dehydrated. Taking the wrong path had ruined the pleasure of the afternoon.

Life can be like a hiking trip. We start on the right path. The wrong path looks deceivingly similar and inviting, but it can turn into a nightmare. We may choose the wrong path innocently enough. By the time we realize what we have done, we are hopelessly lost and in trouble.

The Pocket Full of Quarters website *www.pocketfullofquarters.com* contains a journey map. As I moved to a new state, I would update the website map. People can click on *Journey Map* and follow a little car through the United States. Someone following the journey looked at the map and realized I was heading towards her daughter. She e-mailed, asking if I would make a stop. I called twenty-year-old Jamie and, surprisingly, she accepted the invitation to spend a couple of days together.

As we visited, Jamie poured out her life story. She was homesick and living with a boyfriend who was injured and unable to work. How had she gotten to this point? At age fourteen, she was in gifted classes and making A's. Her future seemed bright. One party offered the opportunity to experiment with alcohol. The next offered drugs. Before she knew it, she had lost interest in school, dropped out, and moved from party to party.

As we talked, Jamie made some decisions. She decided to leave her boyfriend, return home, and re-enroll in school. I shared with her my love for the Lord and the Bible, but she focused on the actions she could take to improve her life. She followed her plan, which worked for a while. There is an old saying, "If you always do what you always did, you always get what you always got." She also continued to party, and eventually the same pattern reoccurred. At the writing of this book, Jamie has dropped out of school again. She is under treatment for depression and not understanding what is wrong with her life.

Psalms 119:104 says we gain understanding by studying God's precepts. It goes on to say that when we have understanding, we will hate every wrong path. How can Jamie change paths? She can seek understanding and develop a hatred for the path that has led her through so much hell.

When I slept alone in a tent, I often wished I had someone standing guard. I now camp with a dog that is quick to wake up at the slightest noise. I sleep easier. Life is full of surprises. Some are good, but many are awful. Our hearts need a guard as we face our lives. For that protection, we turn to Proverbs 2:11 and read that understanding will stand guard for us.

The first stop of Pocket Full of Quarters was a visit with my fifty-three-year-old cousin who was in a hospital in Columbus, Georgia. I walked into the hospital room and quickly backed out. Doug had a mask on. He was thinner than when I'd last seen him. There were wires everywhere. I thought I was in the wrong room until I heard him weakly call, "Cheryle." He removed his mask. "Come in."

I spent the afternoon visiting with Doug, his family, and his pastor, Brother Jimmy.

Since it was Wednesday, Brother Jimmy invited me to a prayer meeting at Faith Baptist Church in Woodbury, Georgia. There were only eight in the service that night, half of them related to Doug.

When I came in, Brother Jimmy introduced me. I sat down and watched as they caught up with each other's lives. "Where are you from?" someone asked. "How long will you be here?" another asked. "I am so sorry about Doug," a member offered comfortingly. "We love him. He leads our music, you know."

"Cheryle will be traveling all over the country," Brother Jimmy explained. Suddenly, I was the center of attention. It turns out that many people fantasize about traveling the country.

"Is your husband going?" a woman asked. "How can you travel by yourself?" a church member fretted. "I can't believe your husband is letting you do this," an incredulous voice responded. I tried to assure them that I had my husband's and God's blessing for this excursion. They worked hard to believe that God would call a woman on such an adventure. This response of love, interest, and reservation was to become familiar over the next few months.

Everyone was surprised as Doug's parents and sister walked into the prayer service. "We couldn't let Cheryle come by herself," Uncle Preston boomed. Cousin Luann walked to the piano, and the service began with singing. The rafters shook with their deep southern accents. I thought of Psalms 98:4 as they made a joyful and loud noise unto the Lord.

Brother Jimmy began listing prayer needs. "Doug is very sick. We need to pray for his wife, Karin. She's still at the hospital. Pray for Cheryle's safety as she travels." He turned to the person on the front row and said, "You begin. I expect everyone to take their turn, and I will end it." No one argued.

I was reminded of the old-fashioned Baptist prayer services of my childhood. I let the sweet intimacy of the small fellowship envelop me. Every person prayed for Doug and his family. "God, help my daughter. I think she is in trouble," a member begged. "Help my husband. He needs to know Jesus," someone else cried. I felt blessed to hear a sweet woman pray, "Keep Cheryle safe. Help her husband while he is alone this summer. Help the people she will be meeting." I was to hear many strangers pray for Pocket Full of Quarters over the next several months. I never grew tired of it.

Uncle Preston's humble prayer moved us to tears. "Father, I'm sending you my second boy. I thought I couldn't stand it when I lost my Bill, but you helped me to understand the purpose. It hurts to be sending you a second son, but I'm not gonna question you. What you do is your business. I had so much fun with my boys. I come now asking you a favor. It helped when I understood why Bill had to die so young. Please help me to understand now."

He paused to collect himself. "I thank you for my beautiful daughter, Luann. She is the apple of my eye. I thank you for my grandchildren and my great-grandchildren. I love my lovely wife, Margaret. You have been good to me. Take care of Cheryle as she travels. Keep her safe. Send her many people that need your love. Send her stories of your faithfulness. Give her wisdom as she writes. In the name of Jesus, Amen."

The pastor closed the prayer by asking God for understanding for Uncle Preston. After praying, we sang again. "Cheryle is a musician," Uncle Preston bragged. She and Luann can sing a duet.

"I don't sing," I protested.

"Get over to that piano!" he ordered. I joined Luann at the piano, and we played together and sang. Uncle Preston led us in his favorite hymn, "Amazing Grace." They agreed to sing my favorite hymn, "In a Garden." The pastor and his wife ended the service by singing a duet. We left laughing and hugging. Church members took a Pocket Full of Quarters card. They loved getting the "free" quarter. Some tried to return it, but I insisted that I wanted their pockets to be "full." They laughed and dropped the quarter into their pocket.

The saints of Faith Baptist Church had truly come together for a prayer meeting. "It isn't always this wonderful," the minister's wife reported.

CHAPTER 9

Worthy Women Say Goodbye!

But the fruit of the Spirit is love, joy, peace, longsuffering, gentleness, goodness, faith, meekness, temperance: against such there is no law.

(Gal. 5:22-23 KJV)

Critical to loving God with a healthy heart is experiencing emotions in a Godly way. By the end of the first week of Pocket Full of Quarters, I had my two least favorite emotions: grief and disappointment. Upon leaving home, excitement was the predominant emotion. My plans (I now cringe when I use those words) were to spend one night in Georgia with Cousin Doug and his family and then continue traveling. God demonstrated on the first night of Pocket Full of Quarters that He would be orchestrating the route and planning the schedule. I was getting the sinking feeling that I should toss my beloved PDA.

When plotting the initial itinerary, my husband and I kept a giant map taped to the kitchen window. Covering this map were sticky-note arrows containing suggestions from family and friends. When I looked at the map, the spirit of God urged, "Begin the journey by visiting Cousin Doug."

But God, I was just there a couple of months ago. Doug and I had let the years slip away without maintaining regular contact. *Surely another visit so soon would be an intrusion.* Sighing, I placed an arrow pointing towards Doug's home in Georgia. *OK, God, I'll stay one night.*

Doug had cancer. When I arrived to find him hospitalized and critically ill, the still, small voice whispered, "Stay and be useful." Disappointed over travel delay, I extended my hotel reservation for a couple of days, hoping his condition would improve.

On the third day the awesomeness of the assignment dawned on me. God was letting me be a part of something holy. Doug was about to go home to be with the Lord. As I walked around at midnight seeing people sleeping on pillows and blankets from my Suburban, I thanked God for letting me be useful. As people in the hospital shared their feelings through tears, I knew God was planning the delivery of His message.

Doug was a country boy, a Christian, an executive, a politician, a musician, and a "manly" man. He knew how to give a good belly laugh and how to play like a child. Doug was someone people enjoyed and admired.

While dying, Doug freely experienced and expressed his emotions. "I'm not afraid to die. I know where I'm going. I just hate to leave my family."

Only fifty three years old, Doug occasionally interrupted the dying process to encourage people around him. He overheard us talking about the problems with the starter on the Suburban and lifted the oxygen mask to offer suggestions. He stopped gasping for air long enough to tell his co-worker where the keys were. Often he smiled and said, "I love you." He made jokes with his sister and smiled at everyone who entered.

With tears pouring down her face, Karin, his wife of twenty-seven years, stood by his bed holding his hand. It was heartbreaking to watch her mingle love and grief. Doug's mother, sister, and daughter surrounded him. As I watched them say good-bye, it occurred to me that the way they prepared for this day was to spend their life being worthy women.

The term *worthy woman* comes from Proverbs 31:10-31. This scripture is a road map for women successfully juggling the pressures of family, profession, and community. Because Karin was worthy, Doug trusted her. Karin made decisions regarding his treatments, food, and medicines. Others cared and offered suggestions, but Doug only listened to Karin. Karin accepted her assignment from Proverbs and honored his trust. She brought him "good and not harm," all the days of her life.

When Doug saw me walk into his hospital room, he was confused. He removed the mask from his face. "Why are you here?"

"I wanted to see you again," I answered.

"But you were just here," he gasped. "How can you take this much time away from work?" Talking was a struggle, so I tried to change the subject. He was persistent.

"OK, Doug. I have to tell you. I lost my job. I am passing through here on a trip across America." Doug looked concerned but returned the mask to his face, sank back into the pillow, and closed his eyes. I thought the conversation was over, but he removed the confining mask again.

In a halting voice he said, "Cheryle, I know you think that job was important. You're wrong. It is not important at all. Look at what is happening to me. When this first happened, I thought my job was important too." He took Karin's hand. "This is what's important. Being her husband is the best job I ever had."

Like the woman in Proverbs, all the women standing around Doug's bed are strong and work with their hands. Doug's daughter, Erica, worked on an assembly line wearing steel-toed shoes. In the hospital, she moved beds and chairs with ease. Karin has chronic back trouble, and yet she supported Doug physically through the challenges of his illness. When asked how her back was, she simply said, "I'm not thinking about it." Aunt Margaret works in her yard and is in excellent physical condition. Cousin Luann can repair appliances. Like the woman in Proverbs, these women have "strong arms."

Doug's manager visited the hospital. "Doug is the best worker I have ever had. I wish I could clone him. He is a great leader." The church expressed their love for Doug. On the day of his funeral, the church marquee read, "Doug, we love you." He was "known in the gates." Now Doug is standing "in the gates of heaven" waiting for Karin.

For Karin, smiling at the future is hard. She faces an empty house and a lonely, broken heart. Karin faced this loss with the same strength she faced other changes in her life. She is originally from Germany. "I have been lonely before. My mother died when I was a child. My father immediately sent me to boarding school."

Twenty-seven years ago, Karin moved to America with her new husband and learned a new language. "I was mad at God. I had lost so much. Doug was a Christian and insisted that I go to church. One night, I was singing a solo. I stopped and could not continue. I needed Jesus in my life. I accepted Christ standing on the stage in church. Suddenly, I knew what it meant to be truly loved."

"Are you going to be OK?" I asked.

"My church family will help me. Erica lives next door. My grandson is a joy. I will have love in my life."

Aunt Margaret was losing the second of her three children. "I have a daughter left. Many people don't even have one child. I am blessed."

Cousin Luann, the peacemaker, spoke with the wisdom mentioned in Proverbs. On her tongue was the "law of kindness." The pain of the dying process created natural tensions, and Luann calmed the troubled waters. "Karin is just tired," she would explain. "Mama is exhausted," she said another time. "It will be all right, Big Brother," she assured Doug. She told jokes in the hospital room and honored Karin's position as Doug's wife. She was consistently kind to everyone throughout the ordeal.

Doug loved his wife and "called her blessed." "She is the best wife a man could ever hope for," he announced to the entire room.

Karin gently leaned over to Doug and said, "I love you."

"I love you, too."

Daughter Erica gently cared for Karin. She was protective of her mother. Like the woman in Proverbs, Karin's child "called her blessed."

Doug gently drew his last breath on Friday. Karin's daughter held her as she began to wail. Their pastor led a prayer as everyone freely held each other and cried. We praised God that Doug was with Jesus. Luann left and went outside to let her daughters hold her close. Uncle Preston and Aunt Margaret cried on each other's shoulder. I tried to help where I could.

After spending the last forty-eight hours in the hospital, I went back to the Bed and Breakfast and slept. When I awoke, I needed to worship. I took my bicycle and headed to Callaway Gardens. Callaway is 14,000 acres in the foothills of the Appalachians. Carson Callaway founded this breathtaking garden in the 1930s, and people have been enjoying its wonder ever since.

I praised God for Doug's life as I rode my bike by colorful flowers, emerald lakes, and playful wildlife. I thought about the emotions I had experienced and witnessed over the last week. Yes, I had witnessed strong and worthy women. Part of their strength was their ability to freely feel and express their emotions. These worthy women's hearts were broken on this terrible day, but their dependence on the Spirit of God gave them strength to say good-bye.

CHAPTER 10

If I Only Had a Heart

A time to be born, and a time to die; a time to plant, and a time to pluck up that which is planted; a time to kill, and a time to heal; a time to break down, and a time to build up; a time to weep, and a time to laugh; a time to mourn, and a time to dance; a time to cast away stones, and a time to gather stones together; a time to embrace, and a time to refrain from embracing; a time to get, and a time to lose; a time to keep, and a time to cast away; a time to rend, and a time to sew; a time to keep silence, and a time to speak; a time to love, and a time to hate; a time of war, and a time of peace.

(Eccles. 3:2-8 KJV)

The poor Tin Man in *The Wizard of Oz* was stuck. The rain had rusted his joints, and he couldn't move. After his rescue, he happily trotted after Dorothy in search of a heart.

Walking back from Old Faithful at Yellowstone National Park, my heart was brimming with emotion. I passed eighty-year-old Eleanor who was breathing heavily, bent over her cane. A young man hovered with concern. I offered help. "I've lost my car, and she can't walk any further," he said. I took Eleanor to my car and waited for his return.

"Wasn't Old Faithful glorious?" she gushed, much like the geyser we had just witnessed.

Pocket Full of Quarters

I had arrived just in time to see the first rush of water. As the fountain sprayed higher each time, gasps from the crowd said it all.

Eleanor beamed as she told her story. "I couldn't have children, but my nephews are my children. Mike is actually a great-nephew. I don't know why he likes to travel with me, but I don't argue. I try not to complain too much about aches and pains, or I'll be a bore."

Presbyterian, her family all attends the same church. "It's sweet to sit together on Sunday. We go to lunch afterwards." Saddened, she described the loss of her husband. "He died from a tumor. I can't believe it's been nine years since he left. I'm grateful he's with God." She shook off the pain and brightened. "God's filled the time, so it hasn't been too bad. My family is good to me." Eleanor has passed through the emotional vicissitudes of life with grace.

There is a time and season for everything under heaven (Ecclesiastes 3:1). I witnessed weeping, laughing, dancing, mourning, death, planting, harvesting, healing, tearing down, building, and more. People with healthy hearts moved from one season to the next with grace that comes from a heart that loves and trusts God. Those with broken hearts were still telling the same tearful story years after the tragedy. Their tears had rusted their hearts.

Ecclesiastes 3:2 - Birth vs. Death

Each person has an appointed time to be born and to die. As I write this, I wait for the birth of my grandson. I have such hopes and dreams for him. I want him to know God the Father, Son, and Holy Ghost. I want my grandson to fall deeply in love with God. Naturally, I want him to have a long life, but only God knows His plans for little Noah.

We celebrate our births and dread our deaths. Birth is traumatic for the infant being born. Little Noah is comfortable and warm inside his mother's womb. He grows, turns, kicks, and even boxes. He thinks this is his entire world. Eventually, Noah's world will become cramped and uncomfortable. It may confuse him as his safe home begins to reject him. Life as he knows it seems over. He will not understand the trauma of his launch into his next season. His first seconds in his new world will be cold and confusing as he gasps for breath. Noah's loving father and mother, Chris and Whitney, will be waiting for him with open arms. He will

62

still be able to turn, kick, and box. Soon, he will be able to leap, run, and dance through an entire world.

Death is much like our birth. Our life in this world becomes restricted as our bodies wear out, and this life rejects us. For the Christian, the dying process might be painful, but our new life is waiting. The only route to our eternal home is to travel through the "birth canal" of death and into our Father's waiting arms.

Ecclesiastes 3:2 - Planting vs. Harvesting

I traveled through Nebraska, nicknamed the Corn Husker State. With 77,000 square miles, they are the sixteenth largest state in area. With a 1.7 million population, they are the thirty-eighth largest state in population. There is plenty of room to stretch in Nebraska.

I expected to see the many rows of corn I passed, but Nebraska is more than corn. Most people don't know that Nebraska has its own beautiful Badlands. It's a state of contrasts. A popular saying in Nebraska is, "If you don't like the weather, just hang around. It'll change." Their highest recorded temperature is 118° and the lowest, -47°. Some years they have droughts and others, floods. Agriculture influences much of Nebraska's economy. They work hard and are leaders in conserving and using natural resources. Their growing season is just 165 days a year. They know when to plant and when to harvest.

Ecclesiastes 3:4 - Killing vs. Healing

I toured Manzanar War Camp in Eastern California's Owens Valley. It's one of ten camps that interned Japanese-Americans and resident Japanese aliens during World War II. The camp opened in 1942 after the Japanese attack on Pearl Harbor killed many Americans. It closed in 1945 after processing 11,000 people through this center. Weather conditions were harsh for the people living in the long wooden un-air-conditioned buildings. The temperature was 110° while I was there. On that brown dry earth remain signs of farming, gardening, worship, and death.

War is a time to kill. Thankfully, that necessary war eventually ended. Next came the time for healing. As a part of the healing process, many Japanese-Americans make an annual pilgrimage back to Manzanar War Camp.

Ecclesiastes 3:3 - Tearing Down vs. Building

St. Vincent de Paul Catholic Church in Andover, Kansas, had a dilemma. Their building needed to be replaced. They had enough money to build a new building but not enough to tear down their old one. There was no land available for purchase. What did they do? They prayed. God sent a tornado that leveled their building. God found the time to tear down, and they found the time to build the building. I got to worship there.

First Baptist Church of Lafayette, Louisiana, was perfectly happy with their building, but God had other plans. A fire burned their building to the ground. When I visited, they were rebuilding. We worshiped in the gymnasium.

Ecclesiastes 3:4 - Weeping vs. Laughing

When God sent me to Wedgwood Baptist Church in Fort Worth, Texas, I had no idea of their tragic history. Late for the worship service, I walked in to hear laughter. Hopeful they were not laughing at me, I knew God had sent me to a church that knew how to laugh. The laughter continued after their worship service and into their small group Sunday School Class as people told jokes and teased throughout the lesson. How does a church learn to laugh like that? As I walked outside, I found the answer. First, they learn to weep.

Standing outside the church was a black marbled memorial with the American Flag flying high. I looked at the youthful pictures and strained to read the gold letters. Horror took my breath away. Less than two years before, a crazed gunman had barged into their youth rally and fired a hundred bullets, killing seven of their members, many of them youth. Then he turned the gun on himself. Yes, this church had a time for weeping. When it was time to laugh again, they chose laughter.

Ecclesiastes 3:4 - Mourning vs. Dancing

The Shepherd of the Hills Homestead and Outdoor Theater marks the birthplace of tourism in the mighty Ozark Mountains, located in Branson, Missouri. The outdoor performance of the *Shepherd of the Hills* was the first of Branson's many interesting attractions. It all started when Harold Bell Wright came to know John and Anna Ross. Harold wandered into the area, discouraged with his failing health and his struggling career as a minister and writer. He intended to stay with

John and Anna for one night. He stayed for the entire summer. He returned every summer until he regained his health. John and Anna helped Harold find his faith and learn to "dance" once again. God was able to use Harold in a mighty way. He wrote their story and published it in 1907. His book, *Shepherd of the Hills,* quickly became a best seller. Poor John and Anna became so famous that they had to move. Today the book is the fourth best-selling fiction of all time.

The play, *Shepherd of the Hills* depicts the lifestyle of the people of the Ozarks at the turn of the century. It takes the audience through their times of mourning and dancing. Life was difficult and often tragic in the Ozarks. Weather conditions were harsh, and people died young. How did these people emotionally survive their difficulties? The answer is faith. They turned to God and mourned their losses. They praised God and learned to "dance." At one point during the play, they invited the audience to join one of their dances. I enjoyed dancing in the Ozarks.

Ecclesiastes 3:5 - Scattering vs. Gathering

I visited a church that could not agree on anything. They fought and finally split. Now the community has two strong churches. It was time to scatter.

I visited another church that had been about to close down. There had been two churches serving the same community. One served the African-American community and the other served the white population. Both churches were failing, so they joined forces. They created a stronger body, and renamed it Unity Baptist Church. In St. Paul, Minnesota, it was time to gather.

Ecclesiastes 3:5 - Embracing vs. Refraining

I had never been away from my husband for longer than a week. Talking on the phone is just not the same as being able to embrace hourly. When Bob joined the journey, the time for refraining was over for a short while.

Ecclesiastes 3:6 - Searching vs. Giving Up

Nervously, I climbed on a subway in downtown Chicago. It was getting dark. Anxious to be at my destination, I took the only seat available—beside a young woman with short jet-black dyed hair sticking straight up at different lengths. She had a black studded dog collar around her neck and matching studded bracelets on her wrists. Her pierced eyebrow accentuated her hard, dilated eyes.

"Do you live nearby?" I asked.

She nodded, stooped over, and began staring at her feet.

Undaunted, I continued, "Do you have family in Chicago?"

She offered a malevolent glare and gave a sharp, "No."

"I'm meeting a friend," I nervously babbled. "I'm traveling across America talking to people about God."

Fed up, she straightened and turned enraged eyes towards me. "My family don't care nothing about me. I don't believe in God." I caught a glimpse of vulnerability in her eyes. She seemed surprised that she'd given so much information and quickly went back to staring at her feet.

"I'm sorry," I whispered. "Families don't always do what they should. God loves you and believes in you. I pray that you will one day know that." The stop arrived, and I shivered as I left. Was her family searching or had they given up on her?

Ecclesiastes 3:6 - Keeping vs. Throwing Away

There is a time to keep and a time to toss. Anyone who has cleaned house knows this principle. The difficult part of this scripture may not necessarily be in knowing what to do. I suspect what is hard about this is getting others to agree with our perspective.

Ken Wilson, Bob Touchton, and Dale Gunter were my business partners for seventeen years. It was interesting when we had to "clean house." Computer companies collect a lot of junk. Ken was decisive and loved to throw things away. Liking to be prepared, careful Bob wanted to keep everything. Calm, levelheaded Dale thinks everything through to its logical conclusion.

When I needed a room emptied, I first sent Ken. If Ken went, I could count on Bob inserting himself in the project. With the two of them working on it, Dale and I usually didn't have to lift a finger. On those few occasions when Bob and Ken could not agree, I asked Dale's opinion. Everyone agreed with wise Dale.

Ecclesiastes 3:7 - Tearing vs. Mending

I arrived in Beatty, Nevada, exhausted after the picturesque but nail-biting trip across Death Valley in 120° temperatures. Checking in at the motel, I confessed that I had no idea what to do if the radiator overheated.

The owner smiled patiently. "Come with me." I followed him outside to my car. "Open your hood." He pointed to the radiator cap and something called an overflow tank. He showed me how to flip the top and fill the overflow tank. "Never take off the radiator cap if your car is hot. Use the overflow tank." Vague memories of hot scalding steam spraying from stranded cars surfaced.

We went back inside to the tiny hotel lobby. "I like to drink hot milk at night," I said. "Do you have a microwave?"

"My wife and daughter are in the house out back. Knock on their door. My wife'll be happy to help."

I found my small clean room and unpacked for the night. Exhausted, I almost skipped the milk. Knowing I needed it, I filled a cup and walked the short distance to their home. When I knocked, their teenage daughter cheerfully greeted me and invited me inside. She later admitted that she thought I was a cousin who had recently moved to town. The wife was expecting me and took my cup.

As I walked in, I saw a brown spinet piano on the left wall. I could see into the small kitchen as the wife was heating my milk. "I haven't played a piano for months. Who plays?"

"I do. My daughter plays the flute. Why don't you play for us?"

Eagerly, I sat down. I saw a songbook. "Why don't you get your flute and play duets with me?" The daughter's face lit up, and she ran to get her flute. The songs were unfamiliar, but I managed to figure them out. The sweet clear sounds of the silver flute rang out over the simple chords from the songbook. It was wonderful to be sitting at a piano. I noticed words about life in heaven before our time on earth. Many of the songs were about family values. I recognized the doctrine from The Church of the Latter Day Saints (nicknamed Mormons).

"Are you a Christian?" I asked the mom.

She laughed. "I am, but you won't believe me."

"I make it a point not make judgments about others' salvation. I have a close friend who goes to your church who has shared much about your faith. We have swapped testimonies and lovingly agreed to disagree. We've been friends for years."

The mom and I gave our individual definitions of Christianity. As expected, they were vastly different, but we found a little common ground. That common ground allowed an intimacy that led to a couple of hours of open sharing. Somehow, we even got on the topic of my struggles and recovery from food addiction and how God helped me.

Eventually, the wife brought out quilts. As I stroked the soft colorful tapestries of flowers and birds, I knew she was an artist. "How do you do this? How did you know these different scraps would form something so lovely?"

Again, she laughed. "The trick is to know when to tear it apart and start over." She reheated the milk and took a Pocket Full of Quarters card.

Ecclesiastes 3:7 - Silence vs. Speaking

On one of those romantic visits from Bob, we had a flat tire on desolate western road in 105° weather. What a great time for silence. Bob did not need or want wifely suggestions as he grunted, strained, and muttered under his breath. When he shouted orders, I pretended he had said "please."

Ecclesiastes 3:8 - Love vs. Hatred

God says we are to hate evil and flee from it. While traveling, I would occasionally witness and hear evil. In New Orleans, a man wearing a dress leapt over trashcans, exposing private body parts to innocent children on the streets. I met people suffering from brutality and loss. A woman was raped while her children were sleeping in the next room. I met criminals and addicts, some recovering, some not. I have witnessed drug deals transpiring on the street.

Before Pocket Full of Quarters, I didn't know that drugs can be passed out in those punch-out chewing gum containers or that people who constantly suck lollipops might be using the drug Ecstasy. I felt the presence of evil when a hotel maintenance man looked me up and down and offered to escort me to my room. Since my best friend, Nancy, had insisted my impending murder would be by a hotel maintenance man with duct tape, I was unnerved. I checked out of the hotel without spending the night. Evil is everywhere. God says we are to hate the evil but love the person.

Ecclesiastes 3:8 - War vs. Peace

Becca was sixteen and a summer lifeguard in New York. Seven-year-old Max was her student. Both were Catholic and liked the quarters. Max grinned, revealing two missing teeth. He glibly announced, "Priests are dumb." Becca and I gasped.

"Why do you think priests are dumb?" I asked.

"My mama says so. That's why we stopped going to church."

Knowing there was a story involved but that he was too young to tell it, I knelt to make eye contact. "I guess it's possible that a priest might be dumb, but all of them aren't dumb. God's never dumb. He loves you. I hope you go back to church."

Becca loves church and goes every Sunday. Her face lit up as she described sitting in church with her parents and boyfriend. "Our church has been full since 9/11. I hate war, but I think it has been good for our country. It has brought people closer to God. Anything that does that must be ultimately good."

Sadly, like the rusted Tin Man, many stay stuck in a season or do not recognize or accept when their season has changed. Mary died of cancer at the age of thirty-four. She left a husband, two small children, and a family that loved her. Mary's sisters, Betty and Jean, shared the intimate details of her life and death.

Mary and Rob married young. They were soulmates who spent every moment together, even professionally. Mary was beautiful with dark hair and brown eyes. Like so many young married people, she was focused on her husband and two children. "She was the perfect mother," Betty reported. "She did everything a mother was supposed to do." Mary was Catholic, but her busyness caused her to lose touch with God and faith.

Shortly after Mary's second child was born, she got a backache. "She was not worried. Everyone knew that two pregnancies were hard on the back," Jean said. It did not get better. Mary went to the doctor and learned she had a severe form of cancer. Frantically, she began painful and debilitating treatment. "Nothing seemed to help. We were all frightened."

Betty was worried about Mary's spiritual condition. "She saw no need for God. Knowing she needed God more than ever, I asked a priest to visit with her. Mary refused to see the priest and take Holy Communion. I ached, but I could only pray."

In an effort to save Mary's life, the doctors tried a bone marrow transplant. Both sisters were tested. Betty was a match. "Honored to help, I really believed this was going to work."

Betty tried again to get Mary to turn to God. "You might as well see the priest. I'm taking communion before this surgery, and you're receiving my bone marrow. Technically that means a part of you is taking communion." Her pleas hit home and Mary agreed. With tears in her eyes, Betty continued. "Mary talked with my priest, took the Holy Communion, and made peace with God. The difference in her was immediate."

The bone marrow transplant didn't work. For Mary, "a time to die" came too soon. She said good-bye to her young daughter and son. She left the man that had been the love of her life.

"I could not stand it. I thought my job was to save her. When my bone marrow didn't help, I fell apart. I felt like I had failed Mary," Betty explained. "It was a long road, but I leaned on God." Betty had a family to take care of. For the sake of her family she worked through this season of "mourning" and learned once again to "dance."

Jean spoke up. "I struggled with bitterness. It wasn't fair. We'd lost so much in our lives. Our father died at age sixty-four, only a year before Mary. Our only brother died at twelve of cystic fibrosis. I was worried about Betty. I realized I too had to trust God. Looking back, I know we are stronger because of everything that's happened to us."

"What about Rob and their two children?" I asked. It had been sixteen years.

Betty sighed. "Rob never got over losing Mary. He hasn't been able to maintain a long-term relationship. He's married and divorced twice. The kids are a mess and stay in trouble all the time. Rob is frantically trying to help them, but he doesn't know what to do."

Rob and Mary had a wonderful season of dancing, birth, and laughing. Rob was not ready for a season of "death." He's stuck in a season of "mourning" and "weeping." His children are stuck in a season of "tearing down" and "war." Being stuck has hardened their hearts to the point that they can no longer experience joy. They join the Tin Man in singing, "If I Only Had a Heart."

STEP THREE

Embrace God, soul to Soul

And thou shalt love the Lord thy God with all thy soul.

(Mark 12:30 KJV)

At my brother's home, the answering machine says, "Hello, you have reached the home of the Milligans. We have gone out right now to find ourselves. If you should happen upon us before we return, please hold us there until we can be located. Or, you could just leave a message at the beep." Our society is obsessed with finding ourselves. In the sixties, people began dropping out of society to "find themselves." Like the message on the answering machine, many people I met on the dusty roads of America had "gone out right now to find themselves."

I met homeless people who left home one day in search of adventure. Now they wander aimlessly through the streets of our larger cities in search of their lost souls. Many asked for money. I talked about God and gave a quarter in a card. The Center for Student Missions is an organization through which churches can send their student groups to minister to such people. Based out of Dana Point, California, their mission is to "Provide students with an effective urban-ministry experience that transforms lives, influences churches, and honors Christ" (www.csm.org).

I was able to visit their facility in urban Seattle, Washington, where my nephew Joshua was serving as a counselor for visiting youth groups. Joshua worked with a different youth group every week. They slept on sleeping bags on the floor and spent their days walking the streets of downtown Seattle and volunteering at indigenous ministries and service organizations located throughout the city. One of their assignments was to find a homeless person and take him or her to lunch. It was surprisingly difficult since most preferred money—most likely for alcohol or drugs. What had happened to these people? They started out to find themselves and lost their souls instead.

What do we mean by *finding ourselves?* I submit that what people are seeking when they go in search of themselves is rest for a restless soul. Our modern dictionary says the soul is our essence. It is the spiritual principle embodied in human beings. In short, our soul is our total self. Our essence cries out for fulfillment.

After touring fifty states, I have come to believe that a vast majority of people—Christians and non-Christians—are suffering from soul sickness because they don't understand that "finding ourselves" means losing ourselves for a greater cause. Continual contact with the Holy Spirit is the answer to restlessness.

I must confess to the sin of vanity. I'm embarrassed to admit that possibly the most nerve-racking part of traveling is the need for haircuts from strangers. Cute, petite Britney chattered cheerfully as she cut and colored my dreary overgrown hair. Britney grew up in a small town that depended on a failing mining industry for its economic base. Single, her two children's father was one of the town's many unemployed men suffering from the long-range effects of hopelessness and inactivity. "I always knew he would make a terrible husband, so I didn't marry him," she said.

"He must have been good at something," I quipped. "You made two children with him."

She smiled.

Listening to Britney, my admiration for her grew. To survive, Britney worked hard and put herself through cosmetology school. She competently cared for her two children, a mentally ill brother, an irresponsible sister, an alcoholic mother, and a sickly-but-beloved grandma. Her soul longed for more, but she didn't know where to start.

As we talked, she confessed to feeling the need for God. "I've been going to a Baptist Church. I want my children to have more than I did. Maybe they won't make the same mistakes. I sent them to Bible School, and they loved it."

"Are you a Christian?"

"I'm not sure."

I walked Britney through the meaning of that question. I asked her what she dreamed about.

"I wish I could leave this small town. I want to find a good and kind man to be a husband to me and a father for my daughters. The men in this town are losers or drunks. I could make more money in a big city and have a good life for my daughters. They need a better selection of men than I had."

"What keeps you here?"

She sighed. "Too many responsibilities."

While I was there, she received phone calls from four different demanding relatives. Listening to her tenderly solve their problems was exhausting. Her *essence* obviously included the personality gifts of mercy and service. Unfortunately, without Christ these abilities had become her jailor.

"Who are you responsible for?" I asked.

She confessed that her mother and sister were adults who should be taking care of themselves. Her daughters, brother, and grandma were a different story. Her mentally ill brother was exhibiting violent behavior and was unable to work. He stayed at home all day. Her sister couldn't keep a job and was taking care of her daughters, brother, and grandma. Her grandmother needed more medical care than they could give, so Britney worried constantly. She knew it was best for her brother and grandma to live in a facility designed to meet their needs, but there were no good choices locally. Britney struggled to keep everyone safe, fed, and cared for.

I asked about finances. Both her brother and her grandmother had small Social Security incomes that could fund other living arrangements. Britney made enough money to support herself and her daughters.

By the time the haircut was finished, we had a life plan for Britney that started with asking Jesus into her life. She knew where she wanted to move and committed to look for an appropriate living facility for her grandma and brother. She decided which hair salon to call for employment. She committed to finding a good church and to dating Christian men. We also decided that she would get a Christian female mentor that would help her know what she was looking for in a life mate.

The next morning, I worshiped in Britney's church. I asked some of the Christian women to guide her through this process. I don't know the end of the story, but I visited the hair salon a year later, and she was gone. Since it was the only shop in town, I'm hopeful.

The first twelve disciples were unable to love Jesus with their souls until they understood that Jesus was God Himself. After Jesus' death, they felt lost and cowered in fear. It wasn't until Jesus returned from the grave that they understood. When they witnessed that spark of the Divine, everything changed. Jesus' gift (the Holy Spirit) enabled them to be able to communicate directly with God, their spirit to His Spirit.

We Americans live in a land that teaches us to "be all that we can be." We have no idea who we can be until we witness the spark of the Divine in our lives. Let's see how others have embraced God, soul to Soul.

CHAPTER 11

The Legacy

If any of you lack wisdom, let him ask of God, that giveth to all men liberally, and upbraideth not; and it shall be given him. But let him ask in faith, nothing wavering. For he that wavereth is like a wave of the sea driven with the wind and tossed.

(James 1:5-6 KJV)

Do you have any idea how unsettling it is to be married to a man who claims James 1:5-6 as his life scripture? According to those verses, all we have to do to find wisdom is ask God. You may be wondering what could be unsettling about a wise husband. The problem lies with the second part of that passage. You see, James 1:5-6 has a catch. We only get this wisdom when we refuse to doubt. A man who doubts is like a sea wave, blown and tossed by the wind. To avoid seasickness, Bob refuses to doubt the wisdom he believes comes from God. Try winning an argument against that level of confidence. Because of this scripture passage, Bob has an unshakable faith in his own decision-making capabilities. That is both enviable and frustrating.

Bob applies this wisdom to his business, personal, school, and church life. Those who know him appreciate and benefit from this wisdom. His appropriate nickname in our business was Fearless Leader. Many refer to him as a visionary.

He is a church leader, a recognized expert in his field, a successful businessperson, and a scholar. He credits all to this scripture.

Lest you think Bob is perfect, listen to the "rest of the story." Bob was born with a high IQ. Understandably, he learned to trust and depend on his own intelligence. However, he often failed to recognize the intelligence and wisdom around him. He spent a good bit of his younger life stymied. His interpersonal skills and arrogance created roadblocks that kept him from achieving great success in his career and his personal goals. His quick wit often crossed into sarcasm that wounded and created personal and professional difficulties.

Then Bob found the amazing James 1:5-6. He began asking for wisdom every morning. He decided to trust that God was going to grant his request, and he acted accordingly. I watched him change. He started recognizing wisdom in others and applying their wisdom to his life. His humility grew. Bob became decisive as God revealed his next steps. He developed an understanding of the behavior of others and grew kinder. Others noticed the transformation. Suddenly, he was getting promotions at work. Co-workers listened to his opinions in meetings and accepted his suggestions. Relationships improved. He grew courageous and learned to take risks.

After a church business meeting one Wednesday, a church member asked, "How does one so young have so much wisdom?" The answer is simple. Bob learned God's secret formula. Bob's wisdom has become a legacy for our children.

I was nervous when I first told Bob about the idea for Pocket Full of Quarters. Even to me, it sounded outlandish. Bob understood right away. As we prepared, he never doubted. I, on the other hand, changed my mind daily as I listened to the many objections raised by loved ones. I was like a "wave in the sea, being tossed about." I finally decided to trust God and stop doubting.

While traveling, I asked God what to do at every crossroad. I felt a sense of wisdom coupled with power as God directed me where to go and what to do. Why were people willing to talk so openly? Why were churches so welcoming? I had none of the world's power. I was not a famous author or an important person. In fact, I didn't even have a job. Usually, I was dressed in shorts, sneakers, and a tank top. Pocket Full of Quarters worked because God gave His power to this ministry.

I visited the Mountain High Health Food Store in Cody, Wyoming, and told the owner, Jim Clark, about Pocket Full of Quarters. Eagerly he said, "Sign my book so when you get famous, I will have your signature." I laughed and signed his guestbook. I had my journey completely mapped out when he said, "You have to travel on Highway 212."

"I don't have time," I argued. "That is too far out of the way."

"You cannot take a trip across America without traveling this highway," he insisted firmly. "Charles Kuralt has rated Highway 212 the "Number 1 Highway" in America. Go to the car and get your map." He took a pen and marked the route. God had sent a messenger.

Highway 212 runs through Montana and Wyoming, skirting the tiptop of the United States and occasionally crossing into Canada. The towering, ice-capped mountains and blue frozen lakes were a surprise in June. As I looked down thousands of feet at the vast expanse of God's creation, I felt a compulsion for private worship. I thanked God for the rewards of His wisdom.

For a significant part of the early journey, a persnickety car starter was plaguing my sense of well-being. Turning off the car was risky business in areas with no cell coverage. My confidence in God's wisdom waned when the car refused to start on a narrow isolated road, far from anyone's concept of a cell tower.

Here, I met a lovely couple strolling hand in hand. They had been married only five years. Previously widowed, both had children from their first marriages. They had dated briefly in high school and had lost all contact until they met again at a high-school reunion. They fell in love all over again. How romantic. I missed my husband.

"We are both Christians but attend different denominations. We take turns. One Sunday, we go to her church and next mine. Religion doesn't matter because we all have the same God." As I stood enjoying God's beauty with this couple, I knew that God had purposely slowed me down. Sure enough, when I returned to my car, it started. Highway 212 is Pocket Full of Quarter's pick for America's best highway.

While traveling through Michigan, I entered a small broken-down gas station. I won't ruin your appetite by describing the conditions of some of the restroom facilities I was forced to use. While paying for my gum (I had to buy something) I heard the droning gravelly voice of an older man. When I reached the counter, the young woman turned off a tape recorder. "What are you listening to?" I asked.

"My grandfather," she replied. "He left a family tape telling the story of his life."

While shopping, I had heard part of his story. "Tell me about your grandfather."

"He spent his life in the woods of Michigan. His father was a railroader. He tried that profession but hated it. He switched to chopping wood for pulp. He spent his entire life logging. He met my grandmother at a logging camp when she was just fifteen. They stayed married until she passed away in her 70's."

On the tape, I had heard him wistfully say, "I guess I had a good life." He told story after story of events that happened in the sprawling woods surrounding that area.

The woman continued her story. "He logged in the summer and trapped in the winter. He trapped beaver and shot deer. Once, in the logging camp, he looked around and counted 450 deer."

I wondered where all the deer had gone.

"A group of men visited a cabin every year. They told their wives they were deer hunting. Instead, they had a party that involved beer, gambling, and occasionally women. Grandpappy would shoot a deer for them, so they could cover their story with their wives. They paid him enough to feed his family all winter."

"Once, he had to trudge through the snow to tell a family that a loved one had passed away. A pack of wolves followed him the entire time, but they never attacked. He lived through the depression on a salary of $3.50 a week. It fed his family."

The stories were charming and funny. They painted a picture of the times and the countryside. As the granddaughter described the time, I could picture it. I looked around and in my imagination, the storefronts melted away. I saw a rough rugged country, and a rough rugged man taming it. He had gone to a lot of trouble to make this tape.

What I did not hear was the purpose or meaning of his life. I kept waiting for the wisdom he had to pass on to his granddaughter. There was none. The tape was a series of stories from a man who had lived his life and finally died. "Did your grandfather have a relationship with God?" I asked.

"No," she answered quickly. "I don't know what he believed. He never went to church. I don't really believe in the God stuff either."

"What do you believe in?"

"I don't know. I've never been to church. I don't know anything about God."

When we talked about God, her eyes had a vacant, bored expression. She seemed so hopeless. She has continued her grandfather's legacy, depending on her own wisdom. Yes, she loves the land and works hard, but she expects nothing more from life.

While I was talking to her, I met her fiancé, a man with no spiritual relationship either. I pictured three or four generations later. Her children's children will probably still love and work the land. They will leave the same legacy. They will work, feed the family on a modest income, and die without offering wisdom or hope for the next generation. Their lives will end with the wistful words, "I guess I had a good life." Like the grandfather, they won't be quite sure.

But wait! This young woman has her entire life in front of her. God loves her and wants her love in return. She could develop a relationship with Him that gives her more love and joy than anything she has experienced thus far. She could work hard and love the land, but she could also have God's wisdom. Her life could have purpose and meaning. She could make a tape recording and give the secret to true happiness to her grandchildren. On her tape, she could leave a legacy of God's wisdom.

She took a quarter.

CHAPTER 12

Worship the Lord God

O worship the Lord in the beauty of holiness: fear before him, all the earth.

(Ps. 96:9 KJV)

Perhaps the most life-changing part of my journey was the worship experiences. I worshiped most places I went. I worshiped in churches every Sunday morning, most Sunday and Wednesday nights, and occasionally on other days. I worshiped in Baptist (several different forms), non-denominational, Catholic, Presbyterian, Episcopal, Methodist, and other churches. I also bowed before my Creator at a funeral, on mountaintops, in valleys, in parks, on Indian reservations, and at ancient ruins. I even worshiped while gazing at a mountain stream as I sat in a casino (where I used no quarters). I tried to worship standing beside a flat tire with temperatures over 100°, but my obstinate soul refused.

Part of the discipline of the trip was to worship at every stop. I worshiped with Christian CD's while driving and while waiting on my temperamental car to co-operate. I now know that I can worship while listening to bad music, waiting on a tow truck, hungry, and in dire need of a restroom facility. I also know my worship experiences are not tied to the quality of the sermon.

I have been a Christian since I was eight years old, in church all of my life, and I had no idea worship could take me to such spiritual heights. I stood gazing at the sparkling orange-and-yellow whimsical hoodoos of Bryce Canyon National Park in Southern Utah, allowing my soul to speak to the God that created these spires of glory. *Make a joyful noise unto the Lord.*

I stood staring at the stark desolate beauty of Death Valley National Park, much of which is below sea level, thanking God for those stark and desolate times in my life that had taught me so much. *Yea, though I walk through the valley of the shadow of death.*

I sat in Carmelite Monastery, holding hands with the stranger who had invited me, listening to the pure sweet voices of the cloistered nuns. *Come before His presence with singing.*

I knew God created us for His pleasure and that worship is for God and not for us. As I thought about the pleasure I was receiving from my worship, I was awe-struck by the thought that God was enjoying it more than I was. God created our souls to spend an eternity worshiping Him. When we truly worship our Father, we are achieving the purpose behind our creation. Illness, handicaps, broken hearts, or even broken cars do not have to limit our soul's ability to worship. Perhaps our time on earth is where we learn how to worship. When we worship, we can let go of everything earthly and join our souls with God's in humble adulation, soul to Soul.

Unity is a melodious word. It implies peace, harmony, and a commonness of purpose. Family unity creates a sanctuary where people come together for strength. Business unity creates a reckoning force. America became stronger after 9/11 because we unified. A church that has worship unity has eternal impact.

I was able to worship with Unity Baptist Church in St. Paul, Minnesota. You may have read about them in a magazine or heard about them on the news, but I first heard about them at the Minneapolis Zoo. There, I met a proud church member, Shawn, who invited me to church. I first noticed Shawn as he excitedly showed his children the monkeys. Later, we sat together on the monorail, blowing bubbles to the animals. His children proudly hung my gift of a cross-shaped bottle of bubbles around their necks. When he heard about Pocket Full of Quarters, he insisted I visit his church.

Before Unity Baptist Church was born, there were two struggling churches with completely different names and worship styles. These churches served the same community with one serving the predominately African-American side and the other the predominately white. The pastors met and became friends. God led them to combine their churches and co-pastor the new Unity Baptist Church.

The service began at 10:45. When I arrived, people met and welcomed me. "You must be Cheryle," a woman said as she hugged me. "Come in. Shawn told us you were coming." The church is a beautiful old building with stained-glass windows. Their racially blended congregation had about seventy-five worshipers. The worship style was a blend of both cultures. They had male and female pastors. A woman led this Mother's Day Sunday.

I walked in to hear the choir warming up, and knew I was going to enjoy this service. It began with a "Call to Unity." The pastor led, "Each person is so precious in His eyes that no one is abandoned by God, not even in death." The people enthusiastically answered, "We shall freely and faithfully serve you, O God, with thanksgiving in our hearts."

I felt the spirit of God minister to me as we said my favorite prayer, The Lord's Prayer. During the welcome, I heard the words, "Cheryle Touchton is worshiping with us today. She is traveling all over America talking to people about God. Cheryle, stand up and tell us about your ministry." I gulped. It was early in the trip, and I was still not completely sure I understood my ministry. It was the first time I had heard the word *ministry* applied to what I was doing. I am not often tongue-tied, but this was one of those occasions. I think I managed to give a reasonably coherent description of what I was doing.

Later they prayed for me and called me a *ministering angel*. I smiled since being an angel has always been a favorite fantasy. My favorite book as a child was *The Littlest Angel*. My favorite television show was *Highway to Heaven*. I was heartbroken when I realized that angels are special creations, and I would never get to be one. I liked the term *ministering angel*.

Unity Baptist has traditions. One is that they say to each other, "God loves you, I love you, and there is nothing you can do about it." They had a greeting time where everyone wandered around hugging each other and repeating that phrase. It did not end until everyone had circulated all the way around the room. I was greeted and hugged by every worshiper at Unity Baptist Church.

We began singing and didn't stop until the worship service was over. Even during the sermon, people would spontaneously break into song. Others joined them while the preacher patiently waited until the hymn had finished. I did them a favor and did not spontaneously break forth into song. I delightedly danced with them as we sang. I thought of the scripture where David sang and danced in the Holy Spirit.

Shawn sings in the choir. His brother Ronnie is the Minister of Music. Ronnie is a self-taught talented musician. As a musician, I enjoyed his talent. Shawn and Ronnie's father, Rev. Ronald A. Smith, is also a talented musician. He sat a couple of rows behind me, and I enjoyed his singing as I worshiped.

One of the favorite parts of the service was something called "Joys and Concerns." This is a time where church members say what they feel led to say. Unity believes in letting the Spirit lead. This session lasted until they were finished. People were patient with long-winded speakers and the occasional show off.

I loved the offering. It was a praise and worship service all by itself. We sang and praised God as we were encouraged to experience the joy of giving. I put a roll of quarters in the offering plate.

The sermon, delivered by a white female, Rev. Cathy Cox, was in the intellectual style of the traditional white community. Rev. Cox is a gentle, intelligent, well-spoken, and educated student of theology. I remember the words, "We are to live like we have come from heaven. Not like we are going to heaven." I am still trying to fully understand and apply that concept.

During the sharing I was comforted by the words, "We are a peculiar people. If we are not peculiar, something is wrong with our walk with Christ." I thought of my own life and admitted that Pocket Full of Quarters was peculiar.

I arrived at my car at 1:45 P.M., having worshiped for almost three hours. The only inconvenience was biological. If I belonged to that church, I would have to eat a bigger breakfast and drink less tea. One of their co-ministers, Rev. Ronald Smith, summed up this church as I tried to compliment him about "his" church. "This is not my church. I gave it to God a long time ago." To God be the glory, great things He has done.

The next day, as I watched the shimmering Badlands National Park of South Dakota dance with the changing light of the sun, I experienced the potent presence of the Great I Am. I realized that these special worship moments are a small glimpse of what heaven is like. If we all lived like we have just come from heaven, people would want to take the trip with us. When I glimpse heaven, I want to skip, dance, and sing praises. That day, I settled for blowing bubbles.

CHAPTER 13

Pockets Full Enough to Share

Having then gifts differing according to the grace that is given to us, whether prophecy, let us prophesy according to the proportion of faith; or ministry, let us wait on our ministering; or he that teacheth, on teaching; or he that exhorteth, on exhortation; he that giveth, let him do it with simplicity; he that ruleth, with diligence; he that sheweth mercy, with cheerfulness.

(Rom. 12:6-8)

While I was dutifully writing about personality gifts, an e-mail cheerfully announced itself as it dropped into my in-box. Temptation—a link to a personality test—was but a click away. By taking this simple test, the secrets of Cheryle would be unlocked, and she would find out why she does what she does. This test promised that I would find out how people respond to me. It would reveal my strengths and weaknesses. Maybe God had sent the e-mail. After all, I was writing about personalities. Unable to resist, I clicked.

In thirty minutes, I had told complete strangers intimate details about my psyche. I later got an e-mail calling me "The Chosen One." It reported that I was a free spirit who liked adventure. The exciting part was that it told me that people liked me. For only $10, I could find more about being "The Chosen One." Alas, I had learned nothing new and had made it easier for advertisers to target their sales directly to my in-box. I already knew I was chosen, but I am guessing the test meant something different. Everyone knows I love adventure. Some people like me while others have stopped just short of hiring a hit man.

As a former corporate executive, I have taken and read many personality tests, each having its own categories for personality types. I believe I am qualified to offer the opinion that Romans 12:6-8 contains the best personality categories available to anyone.

The spiritual gifts listed in Romans 12:6-8 are sometimes called the personality gifts. Studying them is a way to know our essence or our soul. The Church at Crossgate Center in Hot Springs, Arkansas, presented me with a set of tapes containing the best Bible study I have experienced on this subject. Their minister, Rev. Chuck McAlister, said that these gifts are our natural God-given talents. They are a personality tendency, and like most personality tendencies, they do good and evil. When we love God and live in the Spirit, our inborn personality leads to one set of characteristics. When we live as children of the world or "in the flesh" these characteristics have quite another effect. This minister went on to say the list of gifts in 1 Corinthians 12 is the manifestation of the personality gifts in Romans 12:6-8.

Prophecy

The gift of prophecy is the ability to speak the Word of God clearly and faithfully. Prophets allow God to speak through them to communicate the message that people most need to hear. Often unpopular, prophets are spiritually empowered to say what is necessary. The word *prophecy* has negative connotations in our culture because we envision soothsayers, fortune tellers, or mystics. The Bible refers to these as false prophets (Acts 13:6).

I met many prophets on Pocket Full of Quarters. I believe the woman who introduced me as a ministering angel was a prophet. She helped me find my purpose for the journey. One man said I was called for a ministry beyond this journey. His words were prophetic. Another said I would write a book. God continually sent prophets to help me recognize His will and to understand His Word.

Service

Servants help people. On my Pocket Full of Quarters journey, servants offered places to stay, helped with my car, and gave advice about camping. A woman bought me lunch while one of my many mechanics tried to fix my starter. A servant stopped and changed my tire in 105° heat. A couple helped with my camping needs and offered me a place to stay in Texas.

Teaching

Think back to a meaningful teacher in your life. My music teacher, Mrs. Joy Warren, taught me to play the piano. The lessons did not stop there. She demanded confidence, self-respect, and standing straight. She allowed no fear. "That's nonsense," she would say when she saw my performance nerves. "Stand straight, walk out there, and play like you are *my* student!" This red-headed woman taught me to pray before I played. She was a formidable woman who demanded admiration.

Exhorting

A person with the gift of exhortation or encouragement is constantly encouraging the oppressed and the timid. Everywhere I went people encouraged me. Pastors prayed, thanking God for my gifts. Strangers e-mailed me to say how much the website or our conversations helped them. Many have encouraged me to continue my ministry.

Giving

The spirit of giving is a spirit of generosity. The generosity of people was overwhelming as I traveled. An owner of a car-repair shop understood the mission of Pocket Full of Quarters and refused payment for his repairs. A hotel gave me a free night's stay. Church members bought me Sunday lunch, and people donated cash for quarters.

A woman named Jody e-mailed me and invited me to her trailer at the base of Mesa Verde in Colorado. She was a former employee of the company I had just left. While I didn't know her, she remembered me. A friend had sent her a link to the website. When she saw I was nearing her area, she sent the invitation. She spent three days and two nights feeding and housing me and showing me the area. She gave up her bed and slept on the couch. We prayed together and talked about Jesus. Jody believes in Jesus but doesn't trust the Bible. She read to me from her favorite book, and I read to her from the Bible.

Jody and her husband were building a large house on a hill that looked up at Mesa Verde. Her husband was building everything himself, so this project was going to take multiple years to complete. In the meantime, they lived in a small trailer with hummingbird feeders outside their door. A recent e-mail let me know that they had finally moved in.

At Jody's home I finished healing from losing my job. She offered unbiased feedback about the company, how she had perceived my role, and the company's values and goals. I felt my wounded spirit healing and my confidence returning. Most stops were for others, but this one was for me. God used Jody to close that chapter in my life.

Leadership

The gift of leadership is critical for our world, churches, and businesses. It is easy to spot those with the gift of leadership because they are usually in front, talking and giving suggestions. Leaders are charismatic. People naturally want to follow them.

My husband, Bob, played a leadership role in Pocket Full of Quarters. He mapped out directions and planned routes. Daily, he kept up with where I was and searched the web for places for the night. He designed the website and led a team to build it. He repacked the car every time he visited and suggested appropriate ways to use traveling gear.

Mercy

If you have the gift of mercy, everyone knows it. The merciful cry—sometimes loudly—over movies, sermons, and their friends. They are tenderhearted and experience deep empathy. Forgiveness comes naturally to them.

My daughter, Kelley, is a large part of the Pocket Full of Quarters ministry. On the first journey, she flew to Seattle and spent a week camping and helping with the ministry. Mercy is her gift. She cries as she listens and reads my stories. She worries about my comfort. She doesn't want her daddy lonely while I'm gone and includes him with her friends. God has called Kelley into children's ministry, and this gift serves her well.

Yes, we are born with personalities and gifts. To serve God, it is important to start with understanding our innate personality. Who are we that God created and how does He plan to use the gifts we were born with? More importantly, as we grow in Christ, our personalities become like Christ. The life of Jesus demonstrates all the personality gifts. The closer we grow to Jesus, the more spiritual gifts we demonstrate and the more God is able to use us. We, the student, should become like our teacher (Luke 6:40).

On a Wednesday night, Laura Belle asked, "How many dinners are you paying for tonight?"

"Only one." I sighed.

Paul and Laura Belle Forsythe have dedicated their entire lives to serving others. At ninety-three and eighty-nine, they were both very active and still driving a car. Laura Belle collected the money for Wednesday night's supper at church. Paul collected the tickets.

I bragged about how healthy they both were.

Paul laughed and said, "I can no longer run. I was out walking and it began to rain. I started running and realized I was still moving the same speed. I told my feet to run, but they would simply not lift. The brain was willing, but the body wasn't. I don't know which day I actually lost the ability to run."

"Do you still go walking?" I asked.

"Of course! I just carry an umbrella."

Paul and Laura Belle met and fell in love while serving God in a Christian Retreat Center in Ridgecrest, North Carolina. They were partners in ministry for sixty-five years. Laura Belle's life of service began as a PK. For those of you that do not know what that stands for, it is a Preacher's Kid. A PK often feels like they live in a goldfish bowl. The entire world watches and judges their behavior.

"I always said I would never marry a minister. Never say *never* or that will be what God asks you to do," laughed Laura Belle. She has spent her life working beside Paul in ministry. "Back then, churches didn't have a staff. I was Paul's staff. I get no stars in my crown for that work because I did what I had to do."

Paul told his story. "I preached my first sermon when I was still in college. I was nineteen. Our campus ministry worked in an underprivileged community. The minister for the worship that night had cancelled. I was asked to fill in. I was scared, but I did it. I realized that night that I was called to preach."

Paul said yes to God. He went to seminary and began preaching in churches. He has been the pastor to many churches in his sixty-five years of service. He also served in missions. He is now retired.

Paul also served our country in the military. "When World War II broke out, I couldn't stay home. I signed up and became a chaplain." He spent much of his career loving and serving the men and women that risk their lives to defend our country.

Laura Belle dryly added, "He asked to be sent near combat. I had to go home and live with my parents."

With tears in his eyes, Paul said, "During World War II, I would often baptize seventy-five men a Sunday. We baptized right in the ocean that carried them into battle. Many of those men never came home. Reaching these men was the highlight of my life."

Paul served God all over the world in the military. He has served God in Okinawa, Guam, in military hospitals, and places with bullets flying near him. He went where people needed him the most.

Paul and Laura Belle have many natural spiritual gifts. They also believe strongly in preparing their minds for service. Paul was on the Dean's list at the University of Richmond. He graduated with a Bachelor's degree in English and Greek. In 1934, he received his Masters of Divinity from Southern Baptist Theological Seminary.

While most women did not go to college in the 30s, Laura Belle went to Charles Madre Business College.

"Prayer is a big part of our marriage," Paul told me. "We wake up every morning and spend one to two hours reading our Bible and praying. We pray specifically and from lists. We pray for missionaries, our families, neighbors, church, and friends. We pray for the entire church prayer list by name." They have even prayed for Pocket Full of Quarters.

I asked Paul to tell me the biggest focus of his ministry.

"Stewardship," he answered without hesitation. "We are called to be good stewards of the resources God gives us. This means our time, money, and possessions."

"Many people want to give but can't. They do not manage their resources well and do not have enough time or money left to give," he continued. Recently, Paul noticed that church members were throwing away the unused prayer sheets. He stood up in the prayer service and asked us not to be wasteful. "Leave them on your table," he instructed. "I'll collect them and hand them out to the senior citizens on Sunday morning."

"It is important to take care of our body. It is the temple of God. My ninety-three-year-old body still works because I take care of it. I need it to serve God. For most of my life, I ran every day. Now I just walk with an umbrella."

Paul and Laura Belle have spent their life on a minister's income. "We have never been wealthy, but we want to know our money is being used for God's kingdom. Tithing is only the beginning of being good stewards."

"Giving starts with tithing, but it doesn't end there." Paul and Laura Belle gave 50% of their fixed income to churches, ministries, and people. They carefully planned their estate, so their money will continue serving God.

Paul says, "You learn to follow God by saying yes to the small things. When you say yes to the small things and see how well that works, you get better at recognizing and following God's voice in the larger things." At ninety-three and eighty-nine, Paul and Laura Belle had pockets that were full enough to continue giving their time, money, and strength for God's Kingdom.

Paul and Laura Belle have the spiritual gift of giving. Not only do they give to others, they teach others how to give. Their gifts do not stop there. Paul exhibits the gift of prophecy when his words point others to God. Both Paul and Laura

Belle exhibit the gift of service at church. Leadership and teaching gifts were essential to Paul's ministry. Laura Belle worked and taught right beside him. I saw their tender gift of mercy as I heard about their work with troubled families. They encouraged me in my ministry.

How does one couple exhibit all of the spiritual gifts? I believe it is the natural consequence of spending a life trying to be like Christ. God gifted them with pockets full enough to share.

CHAPTER 14

Nailing It to the Cross

For though we walk in the flesh, we do not war after the flesh; for the weapons of our warfare are not carnal, but mighty through God to the pulling down of strong holds; casting down imaginations, and every high thing that exalteth itself against the knowledge of God, and bringing into captivity every thought to the obedience of Christ.

(2 Cor. 10:3-5 KJV)

Fort Pickens is the largest of four strongholds built to fortify Pensacola Bay, Florida, against enemy attack. Building began in 1829, it opened in 1834. It was a massive project that took over 21.5 million bricks to build. Built mostly by slave labor, the fort served the purpose of a peacetime deterrent against invasion. Our country used it until 1947 when the invention of nuclear bombs and guided missiles made such places obsolete. In 1976, it reopened as a National Park.

As I walked along the rolling seashore taking pictures of the time-worn red brick buildings, I thought about the many strongholds in our lives. I sat by the ocean, drinking in the humid salt air, thanking God for the miraculous healings in my life.

The word *stronghold* actually means a fortified place or fortress. In the Bible, it refers to those areas of our lives where we have lost control or power over our own actions. We wonder why we did what we did, but we keep repeating the action.

A stronghold could be as minor as fighting a disciplined and orderly approach to housework or as major as being lost in the dark world of addiction.

These are three examples of common strongholds:

Alcoholism

Isaiah 5:11-12 demonstrates the results of alcoholism. The scripture starts with "woe to those who wake up early in the morning to run after their drinks." Anyone who has lived with the results of alcoholism understands that "woe" does indeed come to the alcoholic as the disease roars through like a tornado, leveling everything in its wake.

I met many alcoholics across America, some recovering and some not. Bill had lost contact with his wife and two children over his drinking. He is now a Christian, sober, and remarried, but his first family has never forgiven him. "I have tried to make amends, but I hurt them too badly."

Money

I met many Americans who confessed that money controlled them. Mike's drive to build a business caused his wife to leave him. "I did not realize what I was doing until it was too late," he said.

Sandy was in a deep depression because she found out that the property she sold immediately resold for more money. "I feel so stupid. I should have set the price higher."

John ruined a family vacation because his daughter lost his wallet. "I don't know why that made me so angry. I just could not let it go."

Robert took a family vacation and ruined it by complaining every time his wife spent money. His wife told the story.

Perhaps all of these people need to pray the prayer in Proverbs 30:8-9, "Please do not make me too rich or too poor. Give me enough to meet my daily needs. If I have too much, I may forget that you are my true God. If I become too poor, I might steal and dishonor your name."

Gluttony

Be not among winebibbers; among riotous eaters of flesh: For the drunkard and the glutton shall come to poverty: and drowsiness shall clothe a man with rags.

(Prov. 23:20-21 KJV)

Like alcohol, gluttony destroys lives. Unlike the alcoholic, the glutton is almost respectable since our society jokes about the problem, offers mouth-watering treats, and encourages the obese to "develop a better body image."

In Rock City, I met a rotund man inching his way through Fat Man's Squeeze. I agonized while watching him hold the many layers of flesh surrounding his stomach and laboriously squeezing it through the turns of the tiny space. Embarrassed, he apologized for the delay. Sadly, I understood his pain. In my twenties, I was grossly obese. Only by the grace of God was I hiking that trail, healthy and whole. As we walked, I shared my recovery with him.

Amy is the daughter of a Baptist minister. She said, "I grew up surrounded by the love of my family and church. I became a Christian when I was a child. I was protected and naïve when I went off to college." As Amy talked in a quiet sweet voice, looking with wide beautiful brown eyes, I could visualize her loving home. Her shining shortly-cropped brown hair shaped a radiant face that looked younger than her thirty years.

What was hard to visualize was the rest of her story. "When I went to college, I wandered away from church and my faith. I wasn't worried. No one around me was going to church either.

"I took a required class on feminine studies designed to expand our horizons and make us more open-minded. As I learned about all of the alternatives to Christianity, I began to doubt my faith. Then we learned about Wicca. Some of us began practicing witchcraft.

"I gained weight and grew terrified. I used bulimia as a form of weight control. I began the pattern of overeating, purging, starving, and then overeating again." She also started drinking and hanging out in bars. "My parents were horrified when

I began tending bars in the most dangerous areas of the city. I walked the inner city streets at night and became friends with gang members. They offered protection in exchange for sexual favors."

As her life grew worse, Amy dropped out of college. She married and divorced twice. "Neither marriage lasted more than a year. Both husbands were addicts practicing my newly adopted lifestyle. I took many risks when I drank. The biggest problem was the bulimia. I began heavily overeating and was terrified to gain weight. I got to the point where food wouldn't stay down. My heart rate was irregular. My stomach constantly hurt. By the end, I had lost the ability to eat and sleep normally."

As her bulimia and lifestyle grew worse, she had trouble keeping a job. "I felt terrible and couldn't make myself go to work." She lost job after job as she became more and more irresponsible.

"I was desperate. I decided that my entire problem was a lost love from high school. I thought I was supposed to be with this man and would finally be happy. Unfortunately, he was married. I didn't care and pursued him relentlessly. Finally, he gave in and left his wife. We were only together a short time before he realized what a mess I was. He told me I needed serious help and then returned to his wife."

The night he left her, Amy's bulimia was at its worst. She was deathly ill. "I wanted to end my life. I saw no way out. Then the phone rang. It was my sister."

Knowing how much trouble Amy was in, her sister had been praying. She was married with two children, both under the age of two. God granted the sister the wisdom to know what to say. Instead of admitting that she wanted to help Amy, she wisely asked for Amy's help. "Amy, I need you. My husband is traveling, and I'm lonely. I need a friend and help with my children. Will you move in and help?"

Amy briefly considered the offer. She knew the rules of her sister's home. Her lifestyle had to change. Her sister would expect her to go to church and live in a manner appropriate for Amy's young niece and nephew. "I had to do something. If I continued my current path, I would die from bulimia or commit suicide. Memories of my childhood flooded me as I remembered what it felt like to be loved and holy. Gratefully, I said yes."

That night, God miraculously healed her bulimia. "For the first time in months, my food stayed down. I slept through the entire night without waking up. God healed me before I ever even started developing a relationship with Him. The act of saying yes to my sister was enough for God. I made that small offering, and He did the rest. I've had no recurrence of bulimia in seven years. I am still an overeater and joined Overeaters Anonymous. Miraculously, I have also been relieved from the compulsion to overeat, one day at a time."

Amy was in church the next Sunday after her sister called and has been every week since. She reestablished ties with her parents and made amends for her past. "One Sunday, I met a sweet Christian man running the sound system. We started dating. Satan made one last attempt. The lost love from high school called with the news that he could not live without me. He offered to leave his wife and marry me. I was at a crossroads. I remembered the pain of my past and struggled with what to do. I told him no and eventually married the sweet man running the sound system. We have been happily married for almost three years."

Amy's husband has a close personal walk with God and a miraculous story of his own. He is a recovering alcoholic and has been alcohol-free for nine years. He is active in Alcoholics Anonymous and helped Amy find Overeaters Anonymous. While God arrested Amy's eating disorder, her emotional reaction to life is still that of an addict. "Overeaters Anonymous helps me to live sanely. It let me out of hell, so church could open the doors of heaven."

Today Amy has an ongoing relationship with God. "Jesus is my best friend. The prayers of my family protected me until I could find Him again." She currently has a job where many depend on her. "God gave me the confidence and ability to perform this job. He took my mistakes and nailed them to the cross. He forgave me and doesn't even remember my past" (Hebrews 8:12).

CHAPTER 15

The Voice in the Wind

And he said, "Go forth, and stand upon the mount before the Lord." And, behold, the Lord passed by, and a great and strong wind rent the mountains, and brake in pieces the rocks before the Lord; but the Lord was not in the wind; and after the wind an earthquake; but the Lord was not in the earthquake; and after the earthquake a fire; but the Lord was not in the fire; and after the fire a still small voice.

(1 Kings 19:11-12 KJV)

*M*ost people I meet tell me they have trouble hearing the voice of God. Christians use the Bible, but when the answers are not directly in the Bible, they admit that they long to hear Him more clearly. Numerous people believe that God is not involved in the details of their lives, so they do not expect frequent dialogue with Him. Some non-Christians believe in a universal higher being who does not make personal contact. A few confess that they see God as a terrorist, and they are afraid to hear Him. Surprisingly few do not believe in God at all and make no effort to hear His voice. I have come to believe that the single biggest problem facing Christians in America is the lack of clear communication with God.

God blessed me with this time where I could put aside all worldly concerns and do nothing but to seek and follow His voice. I was stripped of human support systems and most of the material possessions that require time and attention. I was no less busy than other times in my life, but I knew the freedom that comes from continually hearing and responding to the voice of God. Pocket Full of Quarters is my mountain-top experience.

Listen for the Still, Small Voice

Perhaps the sweetest way we hear a fresh word from God is through the "still, small voice." For most, this elusive voice of the Holy Spirit is what people may be missing when they say they cannot hear the voice of God. We may search for God in the earthquakes and fires of our life, but we will only find Him in the still, small voice (1 Kings 19:12).

My sister-in-law and friend, Louise, told me, "I try to spend time with God every morning. Sometimes I hear the still, small voice right then. More often, I hear it throughout the day. The time with God in the morning raises my awareness of His voice for the rest of the day."

Meditation is how we listen to God. It is amusing to watch Christians bristle at the word *meditation*. Visions of sitting cross-legged and humming come to mind. In a crowded section of the Grand Canyon, I passed a young man sitting precariously on the edge of a steep cliff. Legs crossed in a traditional eastern-meditation position, he was wearing a loincloth and a turban, shirtless with a shaved head.

He shouted, "I am going to chant now." He began humming and chanting nonsense at the top of his lungs. As the sound eerily echoed across the orange-and-yellow plunging crags, I confess to suspecting that his purpose was to attract attention. I have no idea who he was trying to communicate with, but they would have no trouble hearing him.

Use the Bible to Confirm the Voice of God

Hearing the "still, small voice" can be confusing. Satan's voice is deceitful, so we must check out what we hear as God's voice against the written Word of God. A woman named Donna bragged, "God told me to leave my husband. My children were hurt, but I knew I had to obey."

I asked, "Was your husband unfaithful? Did he beat or abuse you?"

"No," she said. "He is a wonderful man. I just did not love him anymore. God wants me to be with someone I love." Donna had not read the Bible, or she would have realized that she had misunderstood that voice. I can say with absolute confidence that God did not tell her to leave her husband and devastate her two children by tearing apart her family. As protection for our family and for ourselves, let's choose to meditate on His word today (Psalms 119:16).

Recognize God's Voice

We have to spend regular time with God if we expect to recognize His voice. Think about those you talk to on the phone. My best friend, Nancy, calls and says, "Hey, it's me." I know her voice because I have been listening to it for thirty-five years. We even communicate with shortcuts. Just last week, she stopped by my house when I was out and left the following message on my white board. "YBFIT-WWW." I knew who had left the message and what it meant. For your benefit, it means, your best friend in the whole wide world.

To hear God, we must first ask Him to speak to us and then be still enough to hear his answer. We hear his still, small voice through prayer, meditation, and Bible study. I asked many Christians if they began their day with God. Most said no. I asked a follow-up question. "Do you hear the still, small voice of God?" You can probably guess their answer.

For me, this is personal. When I was five, my favorite cousin moved out of our town. Lonely and devastated, I sat on the couch every day watching for him to come home. I have always found nature comforting. Across the street from my home was a double lot with a house on one side and a beautifully landscaped yard on the other. If I sat on the couch with my head turned just so, all I could see was a thicket of lush trees and bushes surrounded by blossoming flowers. As I stared at God's tapestry of color, He ministered to my spirit. I went back to that window for years seeking that unnamed comfort that I now realize was meditation. I became a Christian at age eight, but I didn't associate that decision with the peace I found in the window.

As a teenager, I got busy and forgot the art of meditation. I knew about God, but I stopped hearing or feeling Him. While I went to church every week, no one suggested meditation. At twenty-seven—with the help of a Godly mentor—I began practicing morning meditation, prayer, and Bible Study. The sweet relationship that resulted is the driving factor in my life. I never want to go back to being a Christian who cannot hear the "still, small voice" of my Father.

On the Pocket Full of Quarters journey, this "still, small voice" was my constant companion. He kept me safe as He warned me whom and where to avoid. He navigated my trip as He told me where to turn. He prepared the hearts of those I talked with as He told me whom to approach. I sought this voice continually, and He was faithful. I was not always faithful and occasionally paid the price for ignoring this inner voice. In each mistake, I could look back and find where I had ignored the "small, still voice." More importantly, when I did listen I found purpose, adventure, joy, and beauty. My faith grew as I witnessed firsthand the results of following that voice.

Listen To Others

God also speaks through others. My teenage nephew, Bill, has the spiritual gift of prophecy. I know this because he took a test at a youth retreat. I also know because of the words he speaks. Pocket Full of Quarters began with a birthday breakfast celebrating Bill's eleventh birthday. After we ordered, he tore into his two presents. "So… my 'aunt' gave me an 'ant' farm," he quipped. "Waffle House probably won't appreciate it if I put it together now."

I explained that he had to mail away for the ants. "I'm not sure why you can't just get them from your backyard," I told him.

"Aunt Cheryle, those ants might be too small. They could escape. It is important to put the right kind of ant in this farm." He proceeded to give a science lesson about ants. "This summer, I'll have to mail away for my 'aunt' too," he teased.

The Lego watch was another story. Bill wanted to wear it to school. We began the laborious task of trying to put it together. I am not sure I'm smart enough to be a child. On a number of occasions, I was ready to cry *uncle* or at least *brother* on this project. I suggested that we let my husband (his uncle) or his dad (my brother) put it together later.

"Aunt Cheryle," he calmly said, "we can do this." I wondered who the adult was here. Breakfast grew cold as we fought with his new watch.

As we finally got the watch together, guilt washed over me as I remembered my mother's warning not to use teeth for anything other than eating. If you ever have to put a Lego watch together, teeth are critical.

"Aunt Cheryle, what are you going to do if you have to fix your car on this trip?"

"I guess I should call you." I thought about his question many times on the trip as I waited stranded by the side of the road.

Bill was reverent as we talked about what I was going to be doing. He liked the business card containing the real quarter. "Can I have more of your cards?" he quipped. "By the way, how many toys did you pack?" I assured him that I had all of my bubble toys, appropriate stuffed animals, and several other things from my toy box. He seemed satisfied that my "pockets" were sufficiently full for the journey.

Bill loves to say the blessing over food. "Dear God, help Aunt Cheryle find people to give her quarters to. Keep her safe. Oh…and bless the food. In Jesus' name, Amen."

When I returned home, Bill wanted to know what I was going to do next. "I'm going to write a book."

He accepted the answer but warned, "That means you won't make any money for a long time. You're going to have to stop buying toys." For the time it took to write the book, Bill constantly chided me about spending money. At the zoo I started into the gift shop only to be corralled by Bill. When he saw a piano student pay me twenty dollars, he commented, "At least you will have something to tithe with."

Bill continually asked about my book. When he thought I was wasting time, he reminded me that I was supposed to be working on the book. I made a commitment to Bill about finishing the book and missed the deadline. He disapproved, and we renegotiated. I did not miss my next commitment.

Go to Church

God also speaks through church. Martha is the single mother of a fourteen-year-old son. She is worried about him because he has no friends and spends every possible hour playing video games.

"Is he in church?" I asked.

"No. I'm bad," was her sheepish response. "I was raised in church. I just cannot make myself go. I work six days a week and need a day off. I did put him in a Christian school. I hope it helps."

"Don't you need church?" I asked.

"No," she replied. "I already had it. My son needs it now."

As I left her, I grieved for the sweet fellowship she and her son were missing by not belonging to a church.

Use Discipline to Hear God

Would you like some bad news? God speaks to us through discipline. Despite what the sixties taught, actions have consequences. He makes us hear his voice to discipline us. We hear his words from "out of the fire" (Deuteronomy 4:36-37).

A typical Pocket Full of Quarters day began with a breakfast of one egg, two strips of low-fat bacon, and a glass of orange juice cooked on a small electric grill at hotels or a gas grill at campgrounds. After breakfast I had thirty minutes of Bible study, prayer, and meditation and twenty minutes of exercise. Two-hundred miles per day became a rule of thumb with stops every hour for worship, conversation, and ministry. A picnic lunch consisted of meat, vegetables, and fruit. Fruit at 4:00 was a treat.

By 6:00 P.M., I strove to be at my hotel or campground beginning preparations for dinner—which looked a lot like lunch but included a starch of some kind. By 7:30 P.M., I was sitting at a computer working. At 10:00, I stopped for a light snack. By 1:00 A.M., I had put pictures and a story on the website and had researched a route for the next day. I fell exhausted into bed and slept until God awakened me. Occasionally, I ate in restaurants or stayed somewhere multiple days, but that was the exception rather than the rule.

Pocket Full of Quarters would have been impossible without discipline. In four months, I traveled 23,000 miles, wrote 111 stories for the website, and put about 7,000 pictures on the website. God enabled the accomplishment of these seemingly impossible tasks while allowing the time to visit most of the national parks, many state parks, a few amusement parks, churches, malls, people, and national landmarks. His wisdom enabled the discipline it took to make the most of every second. God expanded time and supplied the energy to accomplish His goals.

Watch for Signs

God does speak through signs in the Old and New Testaments. He speaks through signs today. When I returned home, I began attending Christian writer's conferences in an attempt to learn more about communicating the written word. At one low point in a conference when a well-meaning editor made one too many suggestions, I grew discouraged. I was ready to give up on my ministry and this book. I was planning my speech to my husband as I went into the restroom in the conference center. There sitting on the toilet-paper holder were two quarters. I put them in my pocket.

God is everywhere. He is in the wind, flowers, trees, and our souls. His voice constantly calls our name. Crying and lonely, I had just dropped Bob off at the airport in Buffalo, New York, after a romantic weekend at Niagara Falls. I began praying about where to spend the night as I traveled through beautiful upstate New York. I passed one state park and felt God telling me to keep driving. It was after 4:00 P.M., so I ignored Him and pulled in. Naturally, the campground was full. Lakeside Beach State Park, on Lake Ontario, ended up being home for that night.

The first thing I noticed was that it had clean bathrooms, electricity, running water, and showers. I will never take these things for granted again. There was a nice breeze blowing through the campground. The crowded campground had many lakefront sites available. As I checked in, I asked why.

"Well," the ranger drawled. (I thought only southerners drawled.) "It gets pretty windy beside the lake."

"Am I OK in my tent?" I asked.

"Sure." He grinned. Was that mischief I saw in his eyes? "Tonight will not be as bad as last night's wicked windstorm. We're having another one, but it'll be mild." I relaxed. After all, how bad could wind be?

I first tried to put my tent on the open grassy area next to the lake. Down went the ground cover. When I got back with my tent, the ground cover had blown away. At least I caught it before it landed in the lake. Perhaps I should move my campsite back into the protection of the two lone trees.

The next few minutes could have been something from a Three Stooges movie. Every time I left to get something, what I had just put down blew away. When I tried to lay out the tent, it wrapped around me. I stepped on the ground cover and shook out the tent, and they both wrapped around me. As I fought to breathe, I wondered what would be listed as my cause of death. What a humiliating way to end this trip. Would the angels laugh when I got to heaven?

Until this trip, I never knew you could "get the giggles" while alone. There are two choices when tenting in the wind. You laugh or throw a tantrum. Temper tantrums are unfulfilling when there is no one to watch. It is close to impossible to put up a tent in the wind while laughing hysterically.

Neighbors took pity and offered help. Nine-year-old Brooke and her mother, Tina, came to my rescue. Brooke was kind enough to mention, "My cousin's tent blew away last night."

Picturing *The Wizard of Oz,* I asked, "Did you ever find your cousin?"

With a serious face, Brooke answered, "He didn't move but the rain cover moved a long way. We finally found it."

Tina and I talked as we put up the tent. "Yes, I'm a Christian," she answered. "We go to a small church in our area. I teach Sunday School."

"Do you enjoy your church?" I asked.

"I used to. We have a new preacher who preaches fire and brimstone. I'm getting sick of being fussed at."

"What was your church like before this minister?"

"Loving," she answered. "We talked about loving God. What a novel idea. Brooke used to love going to church."

Brooke overheard and offered an opinion. "Our preacher yells at me. He makes me feel bad inside."

Tina sighed. "I probably should change churches. We've visited other churches, but they need me." We talked about the importance of Brooke learning about a loving God. "I would feel guilty leaving. I hate choosing between my daughter's spiritual needs and my church's needs."

"You need to stake down your tent," Brooke informed me. Being a lazy camper, I often skip the stakes. Realizing Brooke was right, I went on a search. She taught me how to put in stakes, so the tent wouldn't move. Brooke did most of the work. By the time we finished, the wind had increased. The tent looked like it was dancing as it moved back and forth rhythmically to the whirring of the wind. I moved the car between the tent and the lake, but it didn't help.

I started cooking and immediately figured out what would stay and what would blow away. The cooler would stay but a full diet coke blew over. Using a tablecloth was a joke. The grill would stay on the table but I had to turn it a special way to keep the fire going. Paper plates and silverware were out of the question. I ate one course at a time, holding hot food in napkins. I thought of the many business luncheons I had attended and wondered what my business associates would think of my dining habits.

Friends and relatives suggested I take a gun on this trip. I listened to them and took a bubble gun. Bear spray is as violent as I intend to get. I enjoyed watching Brooke chase her cousin with my bubble gun. I rode my bike along the white-capped blue waters, talking to God and enjoying the breeze. I set up the computer and wrote for a couple of hours, enjoying the soothing sound of the wind. Sunset lit up the lake with orange, red, and gold hues against a backdrop of blue and white skies. The tent continued swaying as if bowing before the Almighty.

Finally, it was time for bed. As I climbed into the tent, the wind whipped up until it sounded like thunder. The tent and cover rubbed against each other and made an annoying scraping noise. The surf pounded. I wondered if the water's edge had moved closer. As I lay there, I tried to decide what to do.

A strong gust came along and my mattress lifted under me. How did the wind get under the tent? I remembered horror stories about the unleashed power of wind. Doesn't wind sometimes destroy houses? I thought again of the *Wizard of Oz*. I knew nothing about Lake Ontario. Was it tidal? My mattress floated...small comfort at a time like this.

At each gust, I held my breath. Would the next one be stronger? Would this gust collapse the tent? I planned an escape strategy.

I tried to remember the parable about the houses made of straw, sticks, and bricks. Whoops. That was the story of "The Three Little Pigs," not a Bible story. I felt the wind moving my walls and mattress. I felt deep empathy with the little pigs as the wolf huffed and puffed outside their houses. I pictured my stucco home and thought that surely it was equivalent to brick.

God, what am I doing in this tent when I have a perfectly good house?

"Cheryle," I felt Him say, "trust me. I sent you here to meet new friends. Tina needed to talk about her church. You needed to hear Me in the wind."

I wasn't listening. It was time to take charge. I thought about my choices. I could pack up and move to a hotel. I could empty my car and sleep in the back. I could move to the driver's seat and try to sleep sitting up.

Any plan I came up with was riddled with troubles. I pictured trying to find a hotel after 11:00 P.M. in the middle of nowhere without cell coverage. On my drive here, I hadn't passed a hotel in hours. Driving exhausted, late at night, lost in New York seemed riskier than staying in the tent. If I emptied the back of my car, I would be sharing my personal belongings with everyone in the campground as they blew away. I briefly wondered if my mattress would fit on top of everything in my car. OK, what about sleeping sitting up in the driver's seat? Uncomfortable at best. That could be the backup strategy if the tent collapsed.

I considered again about the merits of packing up and trying to find a hotel. It was dark. Brooke was safely asleep in her camper. If I tried to take my tent down alone, part of it would not make it home. No matter. I could buy a new tent. After all, I was more important than the tent. The idea was gaining favor. Then I remembered the safety issue in trying to drive out.

Having ruled out everything else, I turned to God. *How about stopping the windstorm, Lord?*

"No."

But you calmed the storm for the disciples, I argued. He asked the relevance of that statement.

The tent found rhythm. It was a little like being rocked to sleep. I love fans. I started thinking of the wind as a giant fan. I knew I had made my choice. God was whispering, "Stay in the tent."

Once I made my decision, I did not look back. *If I should die before I wake...*

As I lay in my tent, snug in my sleeping bag, I thought about our life on earth. Storms blow around us. When we hear the turmoil, we do not know how bad life will get. With each difficulty, we wait, hoping circumstances will get better.

The disciples experienced a storm. They panicked, too. They awoke Jesus. He scolded their lack of faith then calmed the sea anyway. He used the storm to lead people to Him just as He uses the storms in our lives to lead us to Him. Like the disciples, our imaginations run wild as we picture the wind blowing us away. Brains racing, we ponder our options and grow exhausted.

In desperation, we cry to God for help. We argue. We wonder if we have heard Him correctly. Nervously, we snuggle into our sleeping bags and go to sleep, aware of the roar around us. We have a peace that the world cannot understand. We are fully aware that the wind might blow us away, and yet we're safe in God's arms.

The wind continued throughout the night, but I slept amazingly well. Brooke's stakes held. When I got up the next morning, the ground was littered with everyone's camping gear. Excitedly, Brooke ran over. "Are you OK? We were worried that our camper was going to blow over and crush my cousin sleeping in his tent. We made him come into the camper."

Great, I thought. *I wish you had invited me in.*

STEP FOUR

Serve God, strength by Strength

And thou shalt love the Lord thy God with all thy strength.

(Mark 12:30 KJV)

Most of us are exhausted. We scurry from task to task, sending e-mails while jogging, taking phone calls on the beach, and carrying laptops into coffee shops. Mothers hold babies on aching hips while stirring pots and moving money electronically. Sophisticated time-management systems allow harried executives to coordinate schedules and hold five minute stand-up meetings to make critical business decisions. Farmers rush to feed chickens to enable a timely arrival to their 11:00 A.M. Sunday worship service. Teenagers study calculus in the car on the way to soccer practice. Personal electronic gadgets blare during church services, reminding worshippers that there is no rest for the weary. Is it any wonder that America has difficulty finding the strength to serve God?

We look around and see needs, but we cannot find the time to meet them. Time management classes teach us to list our daily tasks, prioritize them with letters A-C, always tossing out the C's. Words like *urgent* and *important* have become buzzwords to describe our struggles with balancing the constant interruptions against what really matters. We read books that teach us how to relax, go to sleep, and find more time. Health food stores abound with energy drinks, supplements, and power bars. The most common complaint I heard while traveling was, "I don't have enough time to do what is important to me."

Step Four to loving God is to love Him with our strength. It is not enough just to think about serving God. There was a time when I considered myself a Willie Nelson fan. ("Judge not lest you be judged!") Yes, it is true. This is a difficult confession because I am a classical piano teacher. The world that embraces Bach, Beethoven, and Handel does not consider Willie a musician. I blame my father-in-law for dragging me to my first Willie concert where I caught his enthusiasm. I affectionately call my cowboy hat my Willie hat. I have not been to a Willie concert since my father-in-law passed away in 1989, but I treasure the memories.

As much as I liked Willie, I often disagreed with the messages in his music. In one of his popular songs, his protagonist lamented over the habitual wrongs committed against the love of his life. The chorus contained the words, "But you were always on my mind." While the words implied love, his actions spoke otherwise. Love is not complete until it becomes action.

It is hard to understand strength until we understand weakness. Ernie was elderly and feeble. He had separated from his wife of fifty-three years and felt that no one cared about him. I met him at a rest stop where he fell twice. I helped him to his car the first time he fell. After I left, he attempted to walk his dog and fell again. He was a tiny person, so this time I half carried him to his car. He could not drive or sit straight in the car seat. He would not accept food or water from me. His car reeked from where his dog had grown impatient with waiting to be "walked."

Someone called rescue while I cared for Ernie. Ernie said he had heart medicine, but when I looked in his bag, the bottle was empty. When the police and rescue came, Ernie refused to go anywhere with them. Neither the police nor rescue had the necessary training to give medical attention. They tried to convince him to go with them. Ernie refused. Embarrassed by the attention, Ernie felt unworthy. He wanted us to leave him alone.

I asked about Ernie's family. He did not know his son's telephone number. He gave me the name and city. Unfortunately, the telephone number was unlisted, and the police had no way to get the number. Ernie refused to tell us how to get in touch with his wife. Ernie said, "I'm just tired. I need to sleep." We all knew better.

Police and rescue reluctantly left. Ernie had a valid driver's license. He had broken no laws. They were not allowed to force him to get medical attention.

They all agreed that he was a driving hazard, but still they could do nothing. I cleaned up his car after the dog and sat there for an hour, watching him. He seemed a little better after sleeping but was clearly not well. I did not know what else to do, so I finally left. I begged him one more time to let me get help, but he refused. Ernie was weak, sick, and alone.

There is a catch to loving God with our strength. It won't work unless we allow His strength to become ours. I met church members worn out and miserable from futile attempts to serve God and the church. "I have to do this. No one else will," one person grumbled. Another said, "My wife stays mad about the time I spend at church." A minister's wife said, "I've stopped trying to have a marriage. When he gets home at night, he's worn out and just collapses in his chair. He thinks the church will fall apart if he takes a vacation. We don't talk anymore. I won't leave him, so I guess I'm stuck." A discouraged ministerial family said, "We work hard. Why don't more people come?"

These people want to serve God but find their strength insufficient for the task. When exhausted and discouraged, if we will cease from striving, let God be God, and back up to Step One for spiritual nourishment, we will feel as if we have wings on our feet. God's strength will become ours.

Never has it been more critical for sojourners with God to allow His energy to replace their waning multi-tasked strength. After learning to love God with our mind, heart, and soul, serving God is the ultimate energy booster. If we make the decision to follow God (Step One), learn to please Him (Step Two), and communicate with Him soul to Soul (Step Three), then God will direct our steps and supply the energy we need. That's when our time will expand. We will sleep, knowing we have served God faithfully, strength by Strength. Then, we will awaken rested and refreshed, excited about the events of our new day.

CHAPTER 16

If I Only Had the Nerve

Be strong and of a good courage, fear not, nor be afraid of them; for the LORD thy God, He it is that doth go with thee; He will not fail thee, nor forsake thee.

(Deut. 31:6 KJV)

When God said to take the first Pocket Full of Quarters journey, I was terrified. Could I be away so long from family and friends? Would I be safe? Worried family members voiced these terrors. "If you leave your husband for so long, he will find someone else." "An ax murderer with duct tape will find you." "Your car will break down." "Your home will fall apart." "You will run out of money if you don't look for a job." "Your resume will grow cold, and you'll never find a job." The list was endless. Bob was the voice of reason in the middle of these terrorist threats. "God has told us both that you are to do this. Trust Him. If something happens to you, you will become one of the honored who suffered for the cause of Christ."

God commands, "Be strong and courageous!" Courage is essential to strength. The lion in *The Wizard of Oz* believed he could be a "lion and not a mouse, if he only had the nerve." This potential King of the Jungle apparently lacked the courage to fulfill his purpose. Without courage, we will never be able to love God with our strength.

I've always dreamed of becoming a majorette. I began lessons in elementary school and practiced every day. I watched young women twirling batons and imagined what it would feel like to leap, kick, and twirl all at the same time. Finally, the time had arrived for junior-high tryouts. My make up, hair, and outfit were perfect. My friends and family beamed from the audience. I was primed and ready. But just before they called my name, my heart began to pound. Try twirling with shaking hands. After years of practice, my courage failed as the front row had to dodge my flying baton. No one was surprised when I didn't make the squad.

Devastated and furious with myself, I cried out to God. Just before the season started, a majorette suddenly moved away, and I got a second chance. It was a miracle. Before tryouts, I prayed for courage. I made the squad and was a majorette throughout high school. My leaps and kicks became expressions of joy because God heard my cry.

You may be wondering what being a majorette has to do with loving God with your strength. Being a majorette opened doors of influence that God used for his glory. Many on the squad were troubled and needed to hear about God. Parties offered opportunities to take a stand for Godly living. God wanted a missionary on the majorette squad.

I wish I had carried that positive courage and strength into my college years, but courage was the first thing to go. I didn't believe I was good enough to make the college squad, so I stopped practicing. I marched in the band and watched the majorettes with deep regret. As an adult looking back, I know that my skills were as good as most majorettes twirling on the fields of the University of Florida. God spoke again through longings, but I didn't have the courage to try.

Without courage, we are like Samson with short hair (Judges 16). Without courage, we are powerless and ineffective in God's kingdom. With courage, we are like Samson with long hair. We can do all things through Christ who strengthens us. We don't need a wizard to find our nerve. We have God.

In 1984, God led us to start a business. We were terrified, but we stepped out on faith. "Be strong and courageous." Bob, our two business partners, and I worked hard, and God blessed the business. We loved the work and the people. For seventeen years, it was our calling, our income, our mission field, and a labor of love.

Using uncomfortable circumstances and strange longings, God demanded major change. We were terrified once again, but we felt Him whispering, "Be strong and courageous." We never put the business up for sale, yet a potential buyer contacted us. God's timing was perfect. Market conditions changed dramatically months after we sold the business, and the technology industry plummeted. If we had hesitated, we would have been unable to sell, or we would have had to settle for pennies on the dollar.

Bob and I agreed to work for the new owners. Again, we worked hard. We traveled almost every day and worked seventy-hour weeks. Again, God spoke through uncomfortable circumstances. "This is not where I want you. Be strong and courageous," He whispered.

But God, I don't have the courage to make changes. I need your help. Please take action. To my dismay, I lost my job weeks after this prayer.

"Be strong and courageous. Cheryle, I want you to take a trip across America, talking to people about me," God whispered.

But God, my resume will grow stale. No one will hire me! What about an income? I don't want to use up our savings. How can I leave my husband? What about safety issues while traveling alone?

"Be strong and courageous," God whispered. "Just obey."

While on the trip, I continued a job search. "Cheryle, I do not want you to go back to work just yet," God whispered. "I have better plans for you."

But God, I have worked all of my life. I need to work. We need my income. Bob wants to go back to school. He needs me to support him.

"Be strong and courageous," God whispered. "Everything will happen in My time."

I shook my head. *Surely, I can't be hearing you correctly.* I got on my knees and asked God to speak more clearly. I got my tea mug and my Bible and went outside by Lake Michigan to see if I could hear Him more clearly. I guess God realized that I was being stubborn and deaf because He acted directly. He sent Jack and Carolyn.

Jack and Carolyn are part of the Senior Citizen RV Brigade (OK–I made up that name) that is marching across our country.

"Are you a Christian?" Jack quickly asked. I smiled and told them about my trip. Because I was troubled, I shared my recent job loss.

Jack laughed. "So, God has other plans for you, does He? I reckon you'd better listen. It's mighty dangerous to ignore God." He went on to tell his story. "We used to sell broiler chickens. We had a big farm and worked seven days a week. On Sundays, we woke up, worked hard, and rushed to church. We sank exhausted into the pews. We had no time for anything or anybody. We couldn't quit because we had bills to pay."

Carolyn interrupted, "I knew that couldn't be God's plan for us, but I didn't know what to do. Jack and I began to pray. Be careful what you ask for."

I laughed. I'd learned that lesson, too.

Jack's boisterous laughter rang out over the water of Lake Michigan. "God answered all right. Our chickens contracted a virus, and we had to put them down. We were chicken farmers with no chickens and no money. God had answered our prayer, so we figured we'd better not complain. We wondered how God planned to meet those big bills we had."

It was as if one person was talking instead of two. Without missing a beat, Carolyn took over. "We thought about getting jobs. I have a high school education, and Jack graduated from eighth grade. We had been in business together for our entire married lives. Who would hire us? Besides, there was no way we could earn enough to pay those bills."

Jack interjected, "God is faithful, but He sure can make us squirm. We had an $11,000 loan payment due on a Monday, and it was already the Friday before. We had no money and no hope of any. On Monday, we expected to lose our land. We kept praying. On Saturday, a stranger showed up on our doorstep. He had a cashier's check for $16,000 and wanted to buy a small piece of our land."

"Normally the answer would have been no. We loved our land. But when God speaks, you have to listen," Carolyn said wistfully. "We accepted it immediately and took the money to the bank. That was just the beginning. Through miracle after miracle, we were able to make every single payment and keep the rest of our land."

Eventually, Jack and Carolyn started another business on their land. It was more successful than the chicken farm. They made more money and worked less. When they were ready to retire, they sold the business. Proudly, Jack declared, "We are quite comfortable. Now our income funds our ministry. We're church planters." They go where God wants them, park their RV, and help new churches get started.

"Cheryle, what's your last name?" Carolyn asked. When I told her she said, "Oh, Cheryle, your name means you are going to touch tons of people."

Jack reached in his pocket and brought out a ten-dollar bill. He said, "God told me to give you this."

I was stunned and embarrassed. I stammered, "You don't understand. I don't need this money. My husband is employed, and we did well on the sale of the business. I'm just fretting about the loss of my big paycheck and worrying about those bills."

"God told me to give you this!" Jack insisted. "I learned a long time ago to always say yes to God."

I gasped. I remembered my morning prayer. I was worried about money. I had asked God to speak louder. "Thank you," I said. "God is trying to tell me He is in charge of my money." I took the money.

Later, I called Bob and told him I didn't think that God wanted me to go back to work yet. Instantly supportive, he began planning for how we could manage.

Sadly, it's possible to make a decision to follow God (Step One), to get our hearts right with Him (Step Two), to come to know Him so well that we hear His voice (Step Three), and then to "chicken out" on doing what He says (Step Four). I can't tell you how often I hear, "I know God wanted me to (fill in the blank) but (fill in the excuse). No one ever said loving God with our strength is easy. Perhaps that's why the Bible says so many times, "Be strong and courageous!" While it may not be easy, following the call of God is worth the risk. Just ask Jack and Carolyn.

CHAPTER 17

A God of Second Chances

Thou therefore, my son, be strong in the grace that is in Christ Jesus.

(2 Tim. 2:1 KJV)

Grace is my mother's name. As a youth, when the preacher would use the word *grace,* her friends would look at her and giggle. *Grace* is a sweet word with many uses. We use it in sentences such as, "He will grace us with his presence." We say grace before a meal. If someone has grace, they have poise or charm. God's grace is divine love and protection that He gives freely to his people. To be strong in grace means that we remember our grace, so our past won't destroy our future. To love God, strength to Strength, we must remain strong in grace.

Sandra and Rick understand grace. Their love story includes miracles, faithfulness, triumph, and salvation. They are in their fifties and have been happily married for nine years. They work, live, pray, and play together. They spend their lives serving God with their strength.

Sitting in their perfectly decorated, posh living room overlooking a golf course, Sandra told most of their story with Rick interjecting occasionally. "We wake up every morning, have our private devotions, and then travel to work together. When we arrive, we pray the Prayer of Jabez and begin our day. We come home at night and cuddle on the couch."

Sandra and Rick constantly looked at each other and smiled while telling their story. They go to church on Sundays and Wednesdays. They love and enjoy their children and grandchildren. They never forget how blessed they are and gladly share their blessings. Sandra housed me for two nights of the Pocket Full of Quarters journey and dragged me to a meeting of the Red Hat Society where I had the time of my life.

This is the second marriage and second chance for both of them. They each have two children from a previous marriage. When they met, this was where their similarities ended. Sandra explained, "I have been a Christian since I was a child. The first years of my life were difficult because Daddy drank and was abusive. When I was six, my mother left our father and us three children. One day, she just disappeared."

This turned out to be a blessing for Sandra because she went to live with her godly grandmother, aunt, and uncle. "I think of them as my family. They loved us. My aunt and uncle were only able to have one child and saw three more children as an answer to prayer. They took us to church. That's where I met Jesus Christ."

Sandra married a successful man and had two sons. "I was living the American Dream and loved my life. We were active in church. I spent my days being a wife, keeping house, and taking care of the children. My world fell apart when my husband left me for his younger secretary."

"OK God, what now?" Sandra prayed. She knew she had earned the right to self-pity. After all, her mother and her husband had both abandoned her. But Sandra is a survivor. Deeply grieving, she turned to the Scriptures. "The Bible told me to put bitterness, wrath, and anger behind me. I was tempted to sink into self-pity, but I had children. I did the only thing I knew to do: I turned to God, and he was faithful."

"I was determined to raise godly boys. Their father had not been a good example. If I let bitterness take over, my boys would suffer. I made the decision to be happy alone. I had no interest in marrying again until my children left home." Sandra remained single for seventeen years. She worked hard and stayed financially solvent. When she met Rick, she had a good job and had almost paid off her home.

Rick chimed in. "I was raised Catholic, but I wasn't a Christian before I met Sandra. I had a college degree and, by the world's standards, was a success. I married a wonderful woman, and we had two children together."

Unfortunately, Rick began to drink. His drinking got worse until he began losing jobs. "I wasn't worried. I was good at what I did and could always find another job. But eventually I had lost so many jobs that I was unemployable. I also became involved with women. Multiple affairs and financial ruin finally caused my wife to end the marriage. It was completely my fault. My children hated me."

After the end of his marriage, Rick's life became even more focused on women and drinking. When he met Sandra, he was selling vacuum cleaners door to door. He was going to bars nightly to drink and pick up women.

Sandra eventually began selectively dating. She smiled. "Everyone tried to fix me up. I finally gave in. I prayed about dating, but my body is the temple of the Holy Spirit, and I promised God I would not be intimate until I was married. Being practical, I also made a list of all the characteristics I didn't want in a man."

Some of Sandra's friends invited her to a singles mixer put on by a community organization. Her friend pleaded, "Please come. I don't want to go alone. This is a community event. It will be nice." Sandra had been a couple of times and didn't want to go again, but she gave in.

"When we arrived, I was shocked. It felt like a meat market. I wanted to go home, but my friends were not ready. I went to a table in the back of the room and sat alone, deciding not to participate."

Rick was at the same mixer. "I was used to bars. This event was entirely too tame for my tastes. I was bored. I spotted Sandra and thought she was the most attractive woman in the room. I headed straight to her."

Smiling at Rick, Sandra laughed. "He began talking, and I quickly told him I wasn't interested. He was charming. He joked and continued to talk like I hadn't said a word. I relaxed a little."

As he talked with her, he said, "You seem different than the other women here."

Sandra knew it was a typical pick-up line but decided to use the comment as a chance to witness. "I am different. I am a born-again Christian."

Rick added dryly to Sandra's story, "That sure didn't go as I planned. I was not sure what she meant by *born-again*, but I decided not to pursue the subject."

Sandra went on to tell him, "I don't like men that drink." Rick had a drink in his hand. Over the course of the evening, she told him everything she didn't like in a man.

"I realized I was a poster child for everything she detested," Rick joked.

Finally, Sandra's friends were ready to leave. "Rick followed me to my car and asked for my phone number. I refused. He wrote his number on a piece of paper, and I promptly tore it up. Rick laughed and continued to pursue swapping numbers. Peer pressure from her girlfriends and his persistence paid off. Embarrassed and wanting to leave, I gave my number. It didn't occur to me to give a false number, or I would have." Sneakiness is just not Sandra's style.

Rick called several days later and asked her to dinner. "I will not date you," was the quick response.

Rick's charming answer was, "This isn't a date. It's dinner. Have you eaten yet?" She was hungry, relented, and let him pick her up for dinner.

The Carriage Room atmosphere was lovely and romantic. Rick confessed, "I wanted to order an alcoholic drink, but I realized that if I wanted to see Sandra again, I should make do with the steak and baked potato."

While Sandra enjoyed the mouthwatering chicken sautéed with vegetables, she felt out of place and didn't want to be with him. "I spent the evening listing everything I didn't want in a man. He finally admitted aloud that he had all of the characteristics on my list."

Rick admitted, "I left there not feeling very good about myself."

Rick continued to contact Sandra, and Sandra continued to refuse to date him. She did reach out to him spiritually. "I put him in contact with my minister. He and the minister spent time together, and the minister told him about Jesus and salvation."

Rick smiled as he remembered. "I kept calling Sandra. Occasionally she would meet me somewhere. She always reminded me that it was not a date while continuing to repeat everything she didn't like about men like me. She was hoping to get rid of me, but I kept coming around."

"I kept all aspects of the relationship on a friends-only basis. I do mean all," Sandra said, emphatically. There was no doubt about Sandra's meaning. Rick didn't even get to hold her hand. Sandra constantly witnessed to Rick.

"I continued to drink heavily, cruise the bars, and pick up women. I knew my life was going nowhere. One night while driving home, I prayed one simple prayer. I asked God to remove my desire to drink. I began to cry so hard that I had to pull the car over. The grief for my wasted life washed over me. I cried for my broken marriage and my children. I cried for the wasted years. I confessed to God and became a Christian sitting in the car. I didn't understand all it meant, but I surrendered my life to Jesus."

"Being sure she would date me now, I went home and called Sandra. She was thrilled, but she said that I was too new as a Christian to have a serious relationship. She said I had to focus on learning how to be a Christian. My heart sank." Rick stopped drinking immediately and began studying the Bible. He also went back to his church.

"Sandra's minister continued to mentor me. I knew drinking was wrong, but no one told me about the sex part. Imagine my surprise when I found out I couldn't have sex again until I was married. Years in Catholic school, and no one ever told me that part. I had no idea it was in the Bible."

Sandra was the only woman he was interested in, and she would not discuss dating yet. "Marriage in the near term was out of the question. I had never been celibate, and now I was facing years of celibacy. I guess it's a good thing I didn't know that before I accepted Christ."

Gradually, he and Sandra began dating. Rick wanted to get married, but Sandra refused. She told him, "I want a waiting period of a year before I would ever consider anything serious. Also, if you have one drink, the deal is off. You have to stay involved in church and active in a Bible Study. I want you to make amends to your former wife and ask her to go back to you. You also have to restore a relationship with your adult children."

Rick listened and sighed, "Is that all?"

"No," she said. "I want you to have a real job and be financially solvent."

Rick did make amends to his former wife, but she wasn't interested in getting back together. Rick's children finally forgave him. He resigned his job selling vacuum cleaners and took a good sales job that led to his opening a local franchise for a national professional business. Gradually, he became financially successful again. He has not had a drink since the night he accepted Christ. He has been faithful to God, himself, and to Sandra since that night.

For a while, Rick stayed an active Catholic. Believing they needed to worship together, he became involved in Sandra's church. Today, he arrives at their Baptist church early every Sunday to be a part of the prayer team. They fervently pray for the Sunday worship. He is a church member, sings in the choir, and loves his church with the confidence of one who is strong in grace.

"We waited Sandra's year. On our wedding day, in front of a large crowd, I sang "Amazing Grace." I was so filled with abundant grace that I wanted to sing to Sandra and God for giving me a second chance. We were not intimate until our wedding night. You know," Rick smiled again, "Sandra never admitted to being my fiancée. I met every requirement that Sandra set, and she still hesitated."

Sandra smiled as she remembered her indecision. "A war between my faith and my intellect raged inside of me. Intellect told me that Rick could easily stumble. I was afraid to trust him. Faith said to trust Rick and God. Finally, faith won. I have never regretted that step of faith."

Like Rick, God introduces us to grace when we ask Jesus to be our Savior. Our job is to be strong in grace, one day at a time. By living in grace, the past stays in perspective, enabling us to use it to love God with our strength. Rick accepted God's grace when he became a Christian. Because Sandra is strong in grace, she saw Rick with the eyes of Jesus, both before he accepted Christ and afterwards. Now, because of grace, they are able to serve God at home, at work, and at church, together as a team.

CHAPTER 18

Are There Cracks in My Temple Wall?

What? Know ye not that your body is the temple of the Holy Ghost which is in you, which ye have of God, and ye are not your own?

(1 Cor. 6:19 KJV)

Being able to hike, ride a bike, and feel good are joys I don't take for granted. In my twenties, I thought I'd never do these things again. The sin of gluttony seduced and trapped me, rendering me powerless over food. I gained a hundred pounds. My once-healthy, active body grew sick and weak. Through the grace of God, I was able to put the excess food down and eat a healthy diet.

Twenty years later, I still live with the consequences replacing God with food. My confused metabolism maintains twenty extra pounds, regardless of what I do. Stretch marks and scars from obesity-induced health issues make wearing bathing suits an intimidating prospect. I do, however, wear bathing suits because I wear my scars with pride. They remind me of the hell caused by poor temple maintenance. My temple has cracks, but today I lovingly care for it.

Not that I'm an advanced hiker, mind you. In fact, I'm pretty wimpy. When I started on the first journey, I limited hikes to two miles on even terrain. By the end of the journey, I could do up to five miles on rougher terrain. I cannot do steep trails, but my temple is growing stronger.

I visit many temples (churches) in our country. Some are elaborate and others plain. Some are downright ugly and worn out. Our body might be a drafty country church, but our job is to be the temple caretaker. God resides in country churches and elaborate cathedrals.

When I met Walt and Grace Peterson they were both in their eighties. Walt is a tall, distinguished silver-haired man. With her gray curly hair and cheerful smile, Grace came just to his chin. Their well-maintained bodies served God on a daily basis. Their home is actually in an Indianapolis retirement community. However, instead of spending their senior years in retirement, this couple started a Bed and Breakfast in Pine Mountain, Georgia.

"We tried retiring but couldn't sit still. God wants to use us. This business is our ministry," Walt explained. I thought about Moses still working for God at 120 years old. Apparently, He doesn't make exceptions for retirement years. Like Moses at 120, Walt's and Grace's eyes "were not weak nor their strength gone" (Deuteronomy 34:7). They still had work to do.

When I arrived at the brown rustic cabins on the top of the mountain, Walt met me at my car. Frankly, I felt terrible having a man his age carry my luggage. "I'll do it," I offered.

"Nonsense," Walt stubbornly insisted as he lifted the luggage from my car. "You are our guest." I knew better than to argue.

Grace was recovering from a broken leg and stood on crutches at the door. "We're going to a church dinner tonight. Would you like to come?" she invited.

"We're Christians," Walt nodded. "We always invite our guests to church."

I told Walt about Pocket Full of Quarters, and he grew excited. He gave me the names of interesting churches across America. He loaned me a tape of his favorite preacher. He offered a copy of a religious article he authored. He suggested people to contact along the way.

In spite of a broken leg, Grace cooked breakfast the next morning. "Grace and I usually serve breakfast together, but I'm serving while she recovers. She still does the cooking."

"What does the doctor say about her leg?"

"She'll be fine. When she gets the cast off, she'll have to go to physical therapy, but she'll do what the doctor says. Grace never stays in bed."

As Walt served me, I gazed out at the lush green mountain view. "May I pray with you before breakfast?" Walt asked.

"Certainly," I agreed.

"I always ask permission before I pray. Only one guest has refused."

Walt is a cancer survivor. Part of his personal ministry is to visit oncology wards and pray with cancer patients. He's a chaplain in an Indianapolis medical facility. (They close the Bed and Breakfast every winter and go home to serve there.) "No one refuses prayer in an oncology ward." Walt praised God for his recovery from cancer. "I was not expected to live. That was years ago. I take my medicine, exercise, and eat right. God does the rest."

As I watched Walt and Grace, I was amazed at the strength I saw. They eat right and stay in good physical condition. "We've worked hard all of our life. Our hard work ensures our strength for the future."

Good temple maintenance is essential to loving God with our strength. The "Temple of the Holy Ghost" has to last for the length of time we are on earth. Yes, our temple wall may have cracks, but it is the temple assigned to us. Since we are not our own, we are honor bound to care for what belongs to God.

CHAPTER 19

No Whining

Thou therefore endure hardness, as a good soldier of Jesus Christ.

(2 Tim. 2:3 KJV)

Three steps must happen before you take a trip with Aunt Cheryle. First, you must be potty trained. Second, you have to know how to swim. And finally, absolutely no whining. When my nephew Bill was four, he wanted to negotiate the steps. He was potty trained but didn't swim yet. "Aunt Cheryle, you could take me on trips with no swimming."

"But, Bill, there is still that no-whining rule. You like to whine."

He considered it for a moment. "OK, I won't whine if you take me on the next no-swimming trip."

I agreed.

The next trip was to Cypress Gardens. The gardens are beautiful in the spring, but the weather is always hot. Thrilled to be going, Bill stuck to the no-whining rule all day. We chased butterflies in the gardens, watched the water shows, and touched every toy in the gift shop. When we were almost to the front of the only line in the park, Bill said, "Aunt Cheryle, I'm thirsty. I want a soda."

"Bill, I'm thirsty, too, but we're almost ready to ride this ride. We will get a soda after the ride."

"I'm thirsty now."

"Bill, the ride is quick. It won't take long. I'm not getting out of this line."

Bill was quiet for a few minutes as he contemplated his dilemma. "Aunt Cheryle, I know I promised not to whine, but I really want to whine."

I hugged him and said, "But you're not going to." Once he made the decision to accept his circumstances, to endure the thirst, and to persevere through the ride, he had fun. He kept his promise, and we both learned a lesson. Whining is a choice, and we can rebuke it. When we give in to whining, it saps our strength. When we refuse it, we are energized.

Job is our model for endurance. No matter what happened to him, his faith remained strong. He lost his family and his health, but he kept working for God. His friends tried to discourage Job, but he ignored them and even confronted them, becoming their teacher. He praised God throughout his ordeal. His story is still teaching us today. We know we have endured when our hardships work for the cause of Christ.

Lindsey is an eighteen-year-old graduating senior. I met her at a Middletown Baptist Church in Middletown, Kentucky. It was Youth Sunday, and the youth did everything. Lindsey was the Youth Pastor.

I have to confess that I felt like whining when I arrived. I was looking forward to a deep spiritual lesson and was disappointed to hear that I would not be listening to the highly recommended pastor, Dr. James Cobban. I almost left and went to the church up the street.

Lindsey is a beautiful vibrant young woman with long blond hair. Her eyes glow with the love of Christ. Her sermon was articulate, intelligent, and inspiring. She spoke to people about hope and the future. She spoke about depending on God for everything, briefly mentioning an illness. People nodded. The congregation knew what she was talking about. How does one so young get so wise? I wondered. Curious, I talked to Lindsey and her family after the service.

"Lindsey was born at twenty-six weeks," her mom said. "She weighed two pounds and fourteen ounces. She had a Class 4 Bleed on the brain. The doctors said she would probably die. They hinted that dying might be best. If she lived, she was expected to be severely brain damaged." She stopped to take a breath.

"We and our church began to pray that she would live. You see before you the answer to our prayers." The mother smiled proudly and lovingly as she talked about her daughter.

Lindsey has challenges to endure. Because of her premature birth, her ventricles aren't the same size. "My head has hurt my entire life," Lindsey said. "I'm always in severe pain. The doctors put a shunt in my head at birth and have replaced it many times. I currently have three shunts."

"How do you stand it?" I asked. "Do you get discouraged?"

"Sometimes," she said. "But I have learned something most people never learn. I've learned to depend on God. I have to or my life would be awful. I consider my headaches a gift."

"She's had sixty-five surgeries," her mother reported. I gasped. That averaged over 5 per year. "She has constant headaches and is on high levels of pain medication. Through it all, she continued with her studies. She's a leader in her church and gives her testimony when asked."

I also talked to Lindsey's father. "Lindsey is incredible," he said. "I would love for you to tell the story of how she depends on God for help. She doesn't complain. She does her best to keep going no matter how much it hurts. Her faith helps others learn how to depend on God. She's an example for all of us."

Lindsey's mother has a prayer request. "Please pray for technology to advance and for them to be able to create a shunt that will be a permanent solution and end her pain."

Lindsey also has a prayer request. Hers is simple. "Pray my headaches will stop."

Since the writing of this story, Lindsey has had four additional surgeries. Her attitude continues to be positive. Lindsey decided to go through a detoxification program in order to face life medicine free. Her mother said, "She has her entire life in front of her and doesn't want it to be muddled by mood-altering substances. She has her good days and bad days but is usually in severe pain. She takes no narcotics. God continues to use her. A couple of weeks ago, she gave her testimony in another church in town." The Vaughan family has an appointment with specialists to investigate new procedures for blocking nerves, and possibly reducing pain.

For years, this family's life has revolved around medical problems. "We moved here and joined this church when we were expecting Lindsey," her mother said. "We lean on the church and get the spiritual strength to endure."

Not only has this family endured, they have soared in the face of these difficulties. Lindsey's mother, Linda, was the youth leader when I worshiped with them. They honored her during the worship service. The song leader gave a testimony about the difference Lindsey's mother had made in her life. The youth dedicated a dramatic presentation to her. None of them could talk about her without crying.

How does a family endure so much and keep such a positive attitude? Having a child undergo sixty-nine surgeries creates overwhelming physical demands for her caregivers. Somehow, they have endured and taught Lindsey where to find the strength to endure. "Lindsey is a miracle," her mother said. "I'm just grateful that God let her live. I remember that every time I get to take care of her."

When asked how she can endure the pain and still serve God, Lindsey quotes her favorite scripture, "I can do all things through Christ who strengthens me." (Philippians 4:13)

Whining saps our strength, reducing our ability to love God with our strength. Like little Bill at Cypress Gardens and brave, beautiful Lindsey, "endure hardness like a good soldier." No whining!

CHAPTER 20

Stay on the Pony

> Not only so, but we also rejoice in our sufferings, because we know that suffering produces perseverance; perseverance, character; and character, hope. And hope does not disappoint us, because God has poured out his love into our hearts by the Holy Spirit, whom he has given us.
>
> (Rom. 5:3-5 KJV)

Perseverance is exercising our strength, one day at a time. It is getting on the pony and staying on, no matter how it bucks. I hiked the perimeter of a volcano in New Mexico. About halfway around, I was exhausted and ready to give up. Unfortunately, the distance was equal in both directions. Sighing, I persevered. I had no choice. At the end of the hike, I felt like I had conquered the world.

God says we learn perseverance through our suffering. From perseverance comes character and from character, hope (Romans 5:3-5). Hope never disappoints because God has poured His love into our hearts by the Holy Spirit.

I experienced all of Romans 5:3-5 on the trail circling that volcano. I was tired and suffering, but I kept going. I met a couple who was also exhausted. Together, we stopped to rest. As we stared across the stunning valley below with its towering trees and colorful wildflowers, we began talking about God. The man was a Christian who had lost contact with God and the church. His female companion was not a Christian. They lived together and faced difficult issues. They were concerned about a child in their life. They suspected it was time to get married, but both come from failed relationships. They were terrified. This trip was supposed to help them sort out their issues.

As I talked about my relationship with God, it stirred memories in the man. "God and the church could help."

"What are you talking about? How could it help?" the woman asked.

Before I could answer, the man spoke up. "We've been feeling guilty. Jesus could take that guilt. Our son needs help. A youth group could give him direction we can't. We need to learn how to live together. Being around other couples who love each other could teach us something."

The woman's eyes widened. She was seeing a new side of this man that she thought she knew so well. God built my character as I watched His work in their lives. God poured love into my heart as I felt hope for this couple.

I don't know the end of this story, but as we left the woman said, "It's hard not to believe in God while looking at this view."

Run to Win

In Northern Lake Michigan, I discovered a marina filled with beautiful racing boats. Designed for speed, each boat was there to win a race. Yet, only one boat would receive the prize.

People are also supposed to persevere to win races. David was discouraged and unemployed. He told me, "My wife and I are worried. I am fifty-three, and I might not be able to find another job."

"Stop talking that way," I demanded. This was personal. "I'm fifty-one. If you are too old for the work force, that means I am, too. David, you are very employable. I have watched you greet several people as we sat here. You dress well, you're bright, and you communicate well." If David believes he's unemployable, he will be. In each job interview, only one candidate gets the job. David needs to "run in such a way that he may win the prize (1 Corinthians 9:24).

Exercise Self-Control

Staying on the pony takes self-control. When I met Sarah, her life was falling apart. She wondered how things could change so quickly. Prior to her difficulties, she had an ideal life. Her husband had a good job, and they were active in a church. She took care of their two daughters. Sara struggled with weight, but she finally decided that nothing was perfect.

Then things began to change. Her husband lost his good job. The only job he could find paid substantially less money. Sarah had to go to work. Her unmarried daughter got pregnant. She and her husband began fighting. Ashamed of her daughter's pregnancy, Sarah stopped going to church. Her eating spiraled out of control, and she rapidly gained weight. She was continually tired, discouraged, and worried.

I met her as I was passing through her city. As we talked briefly, she asked if we could spend a day together. I agreed. My car needed some work, so she picked me up at the car dealership. I hesitated a moment before I entered her car. Climbing into the car of a stranger is disconcerting. I felt God leading me, so I whispered a quick prayer and got in.

As she poured out her tale of woe, I listened and prayed. She had no control over her husband's job or her daughter's pregnancy. However, she could get help for her eating. She could return to church. She could decide to stop arguing with her husband. She could accept what she couldn't change and change the rest. God would grant the wisdom to know the difference. We prayed together.

Sarah was ready to get help. She agreed to go to Overeater's Anonymous and to take steps to abstain from inappropriate eating. She agreed to return to church. She spoke of her love for her husband and agreed to make amends. Sarah and I became e-mail buddies. She kept her commitments. Her life is not perfect, but she found the relief that comes from exercising self-control. Today, she is at peace with what she cannot change. She's happy again.

Focus on the Path

Part of staying on the pony is picking a path and sticking to it. A business that does not plan goes out of business. College students that don't pick majors, never finish school. People that hop from one job to the next become a "jack of all trades and master of none." Focus is essential to perseverance.

I met a couple who travel the country doing odd jobs. They've worked on farms, in restaurants, and on construction sites. They live in their tent. They're dissatisfied with life, but they continue to wander aimlessly. They're "running their race without aim, and boxing in such a way as to beat air" (1 Cor. 9:26-27).

Discipline

Finally, we are to discipline our bodies and make them our slaves. We are to suit up and show up for life, one day at a time. Like the Energizer Bunny, we keep going. We go to work when we want to stay home. We go to church when it seems boring. We wake up and spend time with God when we want to sleep.

I met people that just stopped going to church. They slept in one morning and never went back. "I never meant to stop going," one mother told me. "Now my son knows nothing about church. I've realized he needs it, but I can't get him to go. He spends all day sitting at his computer."

I met Christians who don't spend daily time in meditation, prayer, and Bible Study. One woman confessed, "I just can't get up early. I'm too sleepy. When I get home, I'm too tired and busy."

Nebraska hosts the very first Pony Express building. It is a tiny cabin, luxurious by Pony Express standards. Founded in April 1860, the famous Pony Express was only in business for eighteen months. It closed its doors for good on October 24, 1861. Their mission was to quickly deliver mail across the country. The founders—William Russell, Alexander Majors, and William Waddell—had big dreams that led them to invest $700,000 of their own money.

Their business plan was simple. Hire people and deliver mail. The advertisement for riders said *Orphans Preferred*. Worried about widows, orphans, and grieving mothers, they required riders to be single. Believing the job dangerous, they offered the outrageous salary of $100 a month. They gave each young rider a Bible, insisting they carry it, along with the company-issued gun and a bugle.

Only183 men are recorded to have ridden for this famous company. The riders rode from station to station, receiving a new horse every ten-to-fifteen miles. They rode with discipline, day and night, through all kinds of weather. They blew their bugle, signaling the office to have a horse ready. They typically rode a fifty-mile route back and forth. The mail worked like a relay race with a rider ready to take over every fifty miles. It took about eleven days to get mail across the country.

The tour guide told us that Buffalo Bill began his career as a Pony Express rider at age fourteen. The owners of Pony Express felt irresponsible giving fourteen year olds a gun, but they felt it necessary for protection. They made the riders sign letters saying they would only use the gun as a last resort and to protect themselves.

It turned out that riding was not as dangerous as everyone expected. While stories vary on the number killed, most agree it was fewer than three. The dangerous job turned out to be managing the Pony Express office. Frequent robberies and Indian attacks caused Pony Express to lose count of the number of dead office managers. Hindsight proved the riders were overpaid, and the office managers were underpaid.

A problem with their business model was the $5 cost of sending a letter. Only the wealthy or desperate could afford to use Pony Express. Technology and politics ended the Pony Express in 1861 when Pony Express hoped to get a million-dollar government contract. It never happened. The telegraph—invented in October of 1861—was cheaper and faster. The outbreak of the Civil War also contributed to their business failure. The owners of Pony Express closed their doors with a $200,000 deficit.

The founders of Pony Express were godly men that cared about their people, possibly to their own detriment. They had high hopes and integrity. Our sense of fair play says that they earned the right to be a financial success. After all, they ran to win and had focus. Their riders were disciplined. Unfortunately, their business adventure was fraught with missed calculations, disappointments, bad timing, and losses of money and people. Did they succeed or fail? To them, it must have felt like a failure.

Let's look again. They ran to win. Pony Express is a colorful part of our history that served an important purpose. Families and businesses that moved west desperately needed a way to maintain contact with the East. The owners of Pony Express are now famous and in history books. They made a difference here on earth. Maybe one of those young riders read that Bible and found God. These owners made a difference for all of eternity.

Now that these owners are in heaven and have God's eternal view, they probably smile at their limited earthly vision. God's ways are not our ways. If we love God with our strength, we persevere even when life disappoints us. Our job is to get on the pony and keep riding. Suffering produces perseverance. Perseverance leads to character and character leads to hope. Hope never disappoints because God pours his love into our hearts, preparing us to move to Step Five in our stairway of spiritual growth.

STEP FIVE

Love God's Children, neighbor to neighbor

Thou shalt love thy neighbour as thyself.

(Mark 12:31 KJV)

*H*ave you ever heard the popular expression, "Love isn't love until you give it away"? The final step to having a Pocket Full of Quarters is being able to put God's love into practice with our neighbors. Jesus said the first commandment is to love God. The second is to love our neighbors as ourselves. Hear His words, "There is no commandment greater than these" (Mark 12:31).

The focus of Pocket Full of Quarters is the *Sh'ma*. As I traveled, I realized the fulfillment of the *Sh'ma* is being neighborly. Everyone we meet is our neighbor. Daily, we ask God to teach us to be a neighbor. As He answers this prayer, we begin seeing needs. We want to serve.

As I traveled, God taught me to sing, "Won't you please, won't you please, please won't you be my neighbor?" (from *Mr. Rogers' Neighborhood*) At first, I felt shy. I worried about intruding, but God reminded me that I was a neighbor. People are leery of strangers. They talk to neighbors.

141

I knew little about car repair, but I had a car full of tools. Broken cars became a chance to be neighborly. It took a while, but I finally ran into someone who knew less about cars than I did. Proudly, I jump-started her car.

Malls became a place to look for lost and confused people. I helped several small children reconnect with parents. An elderly woman needed help finding her car. I didn't have much money to spend, but that didn't mean I couldn't shop. I began offering free consulting advice to the shoppers. They took my advice about clothing, jewelry, and toys. Why anyone would take the advice of someone wearing shorts, a tank top, and a cross-shaped bubble necklace still baffles me. I'm embarrassed to admit that I even offered medical advice in a drug store. I also carried groceries and screaming wiggly children. I distracted many a complaining child with bubbles.

Campgrounds offered a myriad of opportunities to be neighborly. A family had forgotten their frying pan and mine was available. Two obviously lost hikers popped out of the woods and onto the road. Were they ax murderers? Seeing no ax, I offered to drive them the several miles to their campsite. Being neighborly is risky and requires prayer. I trusted my instincts and prayed. No risk I took was greater than the one taken by the Good Samaritan who risked his life to help a stranger (Luke 10:30-37).

As I watched people, I could see pain, demonstrated in faces and bodies. If someone were in physical pain, I could offer to carry something or give them my arm to lean on. If they were in emotional pain, I could offer to listen. Often the source of the emotional pain was a spiritual need, and I could offer a testimony of hope or the word of God as instruction. People are hungry for a neighbor.

I sat in my car one morning waiting to go into church. As people began to arrive, I noticed a scraggly thin young man staggering through the church parking lot on his way to destination unknown. As he reached the middle of the lot, he leaned over and began to throw up. Several church members were pulling into the lot, so I watched. Each got out of his or her car and carefully walked around the young man. One stately man, wearing his Sunday suit, stopped and pondered the situation. Then, Bible in hand, he made his way into church without looking back. When this blond-haired boy stopped throwing up, he stood up, and returned in the direction he had come. I realized I had watched too long. He was gone before I could offer help.

Why did none of us help this sick man? I was so busy judging the reaction of church members that I committed the same sin. The Still Small Voice whispered, "Judge not lest you be judged." Jesus said, "Do this unto the least of my brethren and you do it unto me." I had passed an opportunity to be the Good Samaritan for Jesus. Perhaps the others were worried about a contagious illness or getting their clothes dirty. Did they think his illness was a drug-addict's response to a derelict night? Maybe they were just late for church.

When Jesus told the story of the Good Samaritan, it was no accident that He used the Priest and the Levite, men of God, as villains. The Priest and the Levite crossed the street to avoid a stripped and beaten man. The Samaritan was the neighbor. Jesus said, "Go and do likewise" (Luke 10:27).

CHAPTER 21

Our Savior's Eyes

For I will be merciful to their iniquities, and I will remember their sins no more.

(Heb. 8:12 KJV)

Implied in the commandment to "love our neighbor as ourselves" is that we love ourselves. If we don't appropriately love ourselves, then this commandment backfires. I met people whose remorse was choking the life out of them. One man said, "I did something horrible. No one can love me now. My church and my wife kicked me out."

It's impossible for us to love our neighbors until we love ourselves with the forgiving eyes of Jesus. When we have our Savior's eyes, our past stops working against us and starts working for us. God changes our lives and uses our past to make us a neighbor.

Camping on the Oregon coast, I smiled as I heard laughter from the campsite next to me. Two children were playing catch with their father. Later on the beach, they caught my attention again when the father was hovering close to the water, nervously watching these fishlike swimmers frolic.

Later, I met their mother in the bathhouse where the showers had slots for money. Did I mention that I'll never take my free hot shower for granted again?

"Do you have a quarter?" she asked. I laughed and handed her a pocketful while telling her my mission.

"You must tell people our story," Twilene insisted. "God has turned our lives around." Showers forgotten, we stood in the humid bathhouse, lost in conversation.

"My husband Mike and I were not Christians. We drank and took drugs. We still managed to work but spent our evenings and weekends partying." She stopped for a minute to give her daughter one of the quarters.

"When Peter was born, we knew we were in trouble. At night, we snuggled him between us and talked about our life. We wanted to change for Peter's sake and even talked about God. Together, we vowed this was the last day we would drink and drug. The next morning our life began again, with us making the same mistakes.

"We loved our fun sweet Peter so much. His laughter lit up an entire room. We beamed when he took his first steps. When I combed his soft brown hair, and smelled that sweet baby smell, I dreamed of changing just for him. He deserved it." As bittersweet memories flooded Twilene, she had to stop to wipe her eyes.

The year 1994 began with difficult times for Mike and Twilene. Twilene's mother died suddenly. "I couldn't imagine life without Mom. She was my lifeline, my last link to the good and decent life I had abandoned. I felt guilty about worrying her, and I wallowed in it. You would have thought I'd drink less. Instead, I drank more." She shook her head as if to shake away the horror of what she was about to tell. Her tears came heavier.

Months went by as Twilene sank deeper into addiction and depression. "Friends invited us to go camping. I didn't want to go, but Mike insisted that it would be good for me."

Mike and his friend decided to go white-water rafting. "Come with us," Mike pleaded. "It's a calm river. It will do you good."

"You've been drinking," Twilene accused. "I don't feel safe. Besides, I don't want to go."

Mike grew angry. "Fine! You can stay here feeling sorry for yourself, but Peter's coming with me."

Twilene felt a knot in her stomach. "Don't take Peter," she begged. "You've been drinking."

Mike ignored her. "I haven't had that much to drink. Besides, it's only beer, and the river's calm. I'll be right with him."

"Put on his coat," Twilene suggested. "It's cold." Mike got the tiny coat and left with Twilene shouting after him, "Remember to put a lifejacket on him!"

"They were gone so long that I became terrified. I should have gone. I fretted and paced as I waited. Suddenly I saw Mike coming back to the campsite alone. When I saw tears pouring down his face, I screamed, 'Where is Peter?' again and again.

"The river had not been calm. Peter had fallen out of the boat. He simply slipped off the side and disappeared. It took them five hours to find his small body. Bruises on his chubby legs indicated that rocks entangled him. He was wearing his coat but not a life jacket.

"It was too much. I lost my ability to function. I stopped going to work. My drinking grew worse. Drowning in his own grief, Mike couldn't help me. We both blamed him. Mike spent his days at work, his evenings in bars. In my dark and drunkest moments, I also blamed myself. I knew that Mike and I had chosen this dangerous lifestyle together.

"A man who lived in our neighborhood always talked about God. Mike and I made fun of him. We thought he was a little crazy. After we lost Peter, when everyone else blamed us, this man was kind. He even brought me a red-letter edition of the Bible."

One day, out of desperation, Twilene began to read her Bible. "The words of Jesus were in red. I wanted to believe I would see Peter again. I read about heaven. I felt guilty about not taking care of Peter, and I read about forgiveness. I longed for the hope and peace I was reading about.

"One day, I fell to my knees and sobbed. I poured out my guilt and self-hatred. I poured out my rage and blame towards Mike. I asked Jesus to come into my life. I felt His presence as He gave the blessed peace of grace. I knew how good He was as I felt His love. Not only did He forgive me, He has no memory of my mistakes.

"I knew that if God forgave me, I had to forgive Mike. I knew it because I read it in red letters. I asked God to help me forgive Mike and to love him again. When Mike came home that night, love greeted him at the door. He wanted that love, but he couldn't forgive himself. He didn't think he deserved love. He saw the change in me and sensed the relief I found. A month later, he surrendered. He confessed his mistakes and asked Jesus into his life.

"God immediately took away the drugs and alcohol. We've had none since Jesus saved us. We knew that God wanted to use us, so we offered ourselves to Him."

God led them to the local Salvation Army Church. He uses their past to help people trapped by the addictions that were their former jailors. "One woman we work with has it worse than us. Her drinking killed all four of her children. She hates herself and still refuses forgiveness."

Life is not always easy for Twilene and Mike. "We have to listen to God every day. The Devil wants to drag us back into guilt and shame. We were afraid to have more children because we feared we couldn't be good parents. Jesus told us that with His help, we could do anything."

God blessed them with the two sweet children I watched playing ball with Mike. "Going camping again scared us. God might not remember our mistakes, but we do. We don't make much money, so camping is the only vacation we can afford. We decided we could trust God with our memories. We pray during every camping trip, and we really pray when we get into a boat. We also use lifejackets. We pray when our children are swimming, laughing, or running." Tears were rolling down her face.

Her son ran into the bathroom and smiled. "Mommy must be talking about my big brother again. Losing him broke her heart. Alcohol is the devil's drink, and drugs are the devil's food," he reported before running off to play.

Twilene ended her story by saying, "We have scars. Mike will always be nervous when he sees our children swimming. We depend on God minute by minute and talk to Him all day long. We had to learn to see ourselves through the eyes of Jesus. Helping others heals our scars, one day at a time."

Twilene and Mike are spending their lives helping others. They began following God out of desperation (Step One), allowing the grace of Jesus to heal their broken hearts (Step Two). Their scars are deep, requiring them to maintain a daily relationship with Him, soul to Soul, releasing their strongholds into the care of God (Step Three). Each day, they use their strength to help others suffering from the ravages of addiction (Step Four). By learning to love themselves with the forgiving eyes of Jesus, they are free to love others (Step Five).

CHAPTER 22

The Midas Touch

Here is a simple rule of thumb for behavior: Ask yourself what you want people to
do for you; then grab the initiative and do it for them!

(Luke 6:31 THE MESSAGE)

*A*rule is a generalized course of action. We all have "rules of thumb" that
we choose to follow or ignore. One rule of thumb for my family is that if the dog
barks once and stands by the door, we let her out. Occasionally, we choose to
ignore the rule and pay unpleasant consequences. Thirty-plus years of marriage
have taught me many rules of thumb. For example, when Bob becomes grumpy or
critical, responding in kind is a recipe for disaster. A better course of action is to
verbalize what I love about him. That rule of thumb took years to learn and takes
only minutes to forget.

The Golden Rule is a nickname for a rule of thumb given by the Bible. We should
treat others the way we want to be treated. When we truly love our neighbor as
ourselves, we naturally follow the Golden Rule.

The Golden Rule counteracts some of the world's rules of thumb. For example,
"He who has gold, rules" is a common worldly rule that I occasionally forget. An
eighteen-inch snowstorm in Raleigh, North Carolina, reminded me. This snowstorm

took place shortly before God called me to Pocket Full of Quarters. I realize now that He was preparing me for this first journey.

Stranded along with all of Raleigh, my hotel had no food, and the roads were impassable. Apparently, I'm not as quick thinking as others because by the time I remembered the vending machines, they were empty. No one was sharing. For the first time in my life, I went to bed hungry.

On the second day, a grocery store a mile away opened. I asked the hotel about food arrangements and they not-so-politely suggested that I walk to the grocery store. My only shoes were high-heeled leather boots and cloth slippers. The mile-long walk through deep white glittering snow in the below-freezing temperatures was a nightmare. I tried to be grateful for small things. At least I had a good coat and sweat pants. Weak from low blood sugar, I fell multiple times as each step sank past my knees. Familiar landmarks disappeared under the snow, causing a longer walk than necessary. Finally, I arrived. Not knowing how long the snow would last, I bought as much as I could safely carry.

Lugging grocery bags, the walk home was worse. Had they gotten heavier? It was still snowing, and the landscape had changed again. This time, I got completely lost. I accidentally got off the road and ended up in a waist-high snowdrift. Glad that no one was around to see the humiliation, I climbed out and sat on the road. Hopeless, I stared at my soggy sweat pants, sobbed, and prayed. Suddenly, a large 4X4 truck drove up. The news had asked everyone to stay home, so there were no cars on the road. *Can you have mirages in the snow?*

"Lady, do you need a ride?" a deep voice asked. I gratefully got into the truck with a stranger. My Good Samaritan or angel (take your pick) had a truck that was snow friendly.

"I thought people might be needing help, so I decided to drive around."

I cried all the way back to the hotel with him holding the wheel with one hand and gently patting my shoulder with the other. "Lady, you're OK now. The hotel is right up the street."

I asked if I could pay him, but he refused.

When I returned to the hotel, I noticed other guests had groceries. *How did that happen? I was the only one walking to the store.* Knowing the hotel must have helped, I wondered why they wouldn't help me. Was it something I said? I went to my room with my food.

On the third day, some of the roads opened up, and additional hotel staff came to work. The airport web site said "The airport that never closes." A recorded voice on the phone said, "Closed until further notice." Homesick, I decided to drive my rental car eight hours to Jacksonville. Alas, the snow had buried my car, and I was still stuck. Hotel staff once again refused to help.

On the fourth day, I remembered the rule "He who has the gold, rules." I had plenty of money. I went to the same maintenance men who had refused to help me the day before, this time waving money in their faces. They agreed without hesitation and dug me out in under ten minutes. That's when it hit me. The people who had groceries on Day 2 had offered money to the hotel staff. Since walking was the only way to get groceries, the hotel staff wasn't volunteering to carry any more than they had to.

My first reaction was fury. I pictured the letter I would write to this large and popular hotel chain. I envisioned revenge as I fantasized about the TV news exposé. At the very least, I could write a letter to the newspaper. How dare they not care about their customers? How dare they not be willing to help unless I gave them money? Various versions of, "They will be sorry," ran through my head.

There is danger in being judgmental. God began speaking to my spirit. With horror, I realized that I hadn't volunteered to bring food back for anyone else. Like the hotel staff, my ability to carry groceries was limited. Like the hotel staff, I took care of myself only. Ashamedly, I remembered an elderly couple I had met at the hotel. *What had they done for food?* It had simply never occurred to me to offer help to others.

I failed the test of the Golden Rule. My Good Samaritan/angel had been a neighbor to me. No wonder I had climbed gratefully into a stranger's truck. He was suddenly transformed into a neighbor. My behavior had more in common with the hotel staff than with my neighbor. Instead of angry letters to hotels, television, and newspapers, I found myself on my knees, confessing before God.

There is a side story to the snow fiasco. Throughout the ordeal, I used the phone to cry on my husband's shoulder. Bob has faith in God and me. He knows me well. While sympathetic, he wasn't worried. He knew I would find a way to take care of myself. He communicated confidence on every phone call. I hung up mad every time, with both of us confused.

Finally, I called my brother and cried on his shoulder. Vaughan instantly offered to borrow a 4X4, drive eight hours, and pick me up. I would never let him do such a thing, but I was grateful he offered. I burst into tears as I told him, "No, thank you." He endearingly tried to insist.

I called my husband back. "Vaughan offered to come get me. Now I know why I've been mad at you. I wanted you to be my Knight in Shining Armor and offer to come get me."

Baffled, Bob said, "But you wouldn't have let me. What was the point of offering?"

"Yes, but I wanted you to offer."

Bob's next call was to Vaughan. "You got me in trouble. The next time you get the wild idea to rescue my wife, call me and suggest that I make the offer."

Vaughan laughed. "It was a pretty safe offer. We both know she would never let us do it."

Just a few short months later, I was on the road, trying to be a neighbor to everyone I met. What I found was people being neighborly to me. They fed me breakfast, lunch, and dinner. Campers offered cups of coffee, meals, and tools. A child brought cookies. At first, their generosity was a source of discomfort, but slowly I developed the humility to say, "Thank you." By the end of the trip, I enjoyed letting others share with me.

Much of my trip was about batteries and refrigerators. God has a sense of humor and often entertained me by the illogic of the devices he entrusted to me. For weeks, we tried to rig a device that would charge my extra battery during the day and run the refrigerator off of it at night. I use *we* loosely. "*We*" really means that my husband was trying to coach me from miles away.

Despite our best efforts, the battery would not charge. Bob was afraid the wires were loose and that my car battery was not holding a complete charge. He advised me to find someone who could "top off my car battery." Strangely, I understood what he meant. Bob also wanted someone to check the connections on the second battery. I entered a local Midas dealership and babbled to the woman at the counter. She had no idea what I was trying to explain. "The owner is on the phone," was her single response.

I looked over to see a man having a heated conversation. As I listened to him, I heard familiar words. "My computer is not working. Your job is to keep it working. Do you see any problem here?"

I groaned. Experience told me his conversation wasn't going to be good for his frame of mind when he finally got off the phone.

While waiting in the lobby, I struck up a conversation with another customer. She had moved to this small Tennessee town to buy repossessed homes, fix them up, and resell them. She did most of the work herself. Her job involved hammers, plaster, wiring, paint, and lumber. Obviously, this woman would never be in my predicament.

Finally, the owner got off the phone. Feeling like a helpless female, I described what I needed. I could tell the handy-woman sitting next to me was amused. I started jabbering about trips, writing, batteries, and husbands.

The owner smiled. "What are you writing about?"

"I'm writing about people's relationship with God."

Looking me in the eye, he asked, "Where do you stand with God?"

"Actually, I have a close relationship with Him." *Was I feeling defensive?*

He probed further, "What is the name of your God?"

"I'm a Christian." *Who was the interviewer here?*

He smiled again. "Good. There's an awful lot of strange beliefs out there that don't do folks much good. Since you know Jesus, we can now talk about your car." He looked at my car and went to laughing. "Now that's a creative approach to solving a problem."

"My husband is nothing if not creative."

"I'm going to charge your car battery. This electrical tape has melted. I have some tubing here that'll work better." With us talking the entire time, he made covers for both batteries. Since I'm from the computer industry, I probed about his computer problems. Midas was moving all of their franchises to a Point Of Sale system. Now *that* I understood. I started to go into sell mode and caught myself as I realized I no longer had anything to sell. I also realized that without the backup of a networking department, I couldn't even help his immediate network problem. So much for being useful.

In the middle of the work, his wife arrived. "You promised you would be dressed up."

When he looked up, baffled, she laughed. "You don't have a clue, do you?"

He rushed back to his office and asked his secretary, "What did I forget?" Oops. His wife had planned a romantic evening and hired a babysitter. I offered to skip the rest of the repair work and encouraged him to leave with his wife.

"Nope. I need to finish." He was being nice, and I hated that he was in trouble. I went inside to see if I could smooth things over with his wife. "Sorry. I came here at the last minute, and he couldn't turn me down."

"I'm used to it. Of course he had to help you." I told her about my trip. She told me about growing up in a preacher's home. "My daddy and mama love God. Out of six children, five of us also ended up loving Him."

Finally, he was finished. He had done several extra things, so the battery was working again. I will not embarrass myself by trying to explain what he did.

"What do I owe?" I asked.

"That's up to my wife," was his light response. "Depends on what she thinks her waiting is worth."

She smiled. "You owe us nothing. Just enjoy your trip. You're doing God's work."

I argued with her. "This is a business. How can you make money if you don't charge your customers?"

"God takes care of us. We just try to do what he says." She looked at her husband. "Now can you dress up for me? I'll make it worth your while," she promised with a wink and a sparkle in her eye.

I thought of the story of King Midas. Everything he touched turned to gold. By being a good neighbor, these Midas franchise owners are leading people to an eternity of streets lined with gold.

CHAPTER 23

Where is Love?

I solemnly charge you in the presence of God and of Christ Jesus and of the chosen angels that you guard and keep [these rules] without personal prejudice or favor, doing nothing from partiality.

(1 Tim. 5:21 AMP)

Prejudice is the antithesis of loving your neighbor as yourself. To be prejudiced is to have a preconceived preference or idea. It is also having an irrational suspicion or hatred of a particular group, race, or religion (dictionary.com). We are prejudiced when we make up our minds prior to investigation or when we make judgments about an individual based on perceived cultural traits or norms of groups, races, or religions. We are prejudiced when we make global negative statements about any group, race, or religion, or when we hate or hurt a group, race, or religion. Prejudice steals our love for our neighbors and leaves us singing with Oliver, "Where is Love?" (from the Broadway musical, *Oliver*).

Here is where I have a confession to make. At one time, I was prejudiced against those who displayed prejudice. For some reason, I thought the sin of prejudice was worse than others. I have been known to say, "Prejudiced people are just plain ignorant." Do you see any global negative statements about that position? I got into bitter arguments when I heard people negatively stereotyping (and sometimes positively stereotyping) groups, races, or religions. I abandoned friends that I believed to be prejudiced. My faith suffered when I realized a church I attended spoke words of love but refused a specific race entry to their daycare center.

That was when God convicted me of the sin of prejudice. To think all prejudiced people were ignorant was stereotyping. To label people that stereotyped as "prejudiced" was judgmental. To abandon friends because of one particular sin was not walking in Jesus' footsteps. Allowing my faith to suffer because of the mistakes of an otherwise-loving church meant my faith was weak. We don't have to agree with what people say or think but we're always responsible to forgive and love.

If you are prejudiced, don't panic. It is not hopeless. You're in good company. Peter, a disciple of Jesus, suffered from prejudice to the point that it was blocking his love for his neighbors and interfering with Christ's mission. Poor Peter in Acts 10. Jesus told him three times before he finally got the message and obeyed. The light of truth dawned and his confession in verses 27-29 is heartwarming: "God has shown me that no race is better than another" (from *The Message*).

Jim is an average hard-working, church-going, patriotic American. While Jim had grown up Catholic, he actually accepted Christ when he met his wife. He and his wife became active in a Baptist Church. Together, they raised their son and daughter there.

In most areas of Jim's life, he is loving, kind, and considerate. He shared his Christian testimony with anyone who would listen. His face lit up when he proudly talked about his family, both biological and church. In church and his neighborhood, he was quick to offer help to those in need. His natural empathy for those in pain led people to tell him their problems. His spiritual gifts are the popular ones of service and encouragement.

Throughout his Christian walk, Jim has refused to surrender one key part of his life. Jim hates a particular race. He deliberately joined a church made up of people not from that race. When an occasional "outsider" attended, he grumbled. Some church members tried to confront him, but it ended in speeches and arguments.

Over the years, the church matured and grew racially integrated. At the same time, Jim grew increasingly dissatisfied. Racial issues infiltrated other areas of his life, and he became angry and vocal. After he was involved in a racial incident at his son's ball game, the police handcuffed him and took him to the police station.

To his Sunday School teacher's dismay, he turned every Bible Study into a debate over racial issues.

One Sunday, the topic was abortion. The majority of the class took the Right-to-Life position. Jim horrified everyone by stating, "I am against abortion unless the child is racially mixed."

There were so many things wrong with the statement that the class didn't know where to begin. For a moment, they sat stunned. The teacher finally said, "Jim, surely you didn't mean that as harshly as it came out."

Jim angrily replied, "Yes, I did."

Trying to help the situation become more personal, someone in the class said, "Jim, think about what you're saying. If your daughter, Sharon, married a person from the race you hate, surely you would not want her to abort your own grandchildren."

Jim responded, "Yes I would! It would break my heart to know that a grandchild of mine had to live with the stigma of mixed race. I couldn't stand it. I would rather him or her be dead than to have to live with that." There were tears in his eyes. He sincerely meant what he said. The class gave up and moved on. Many in the class began praying for Jim. They wondered how such a loving man could carry so much hate.

Things came to a head for Jim when Benny joined the church. Benny was a member of the race Jim hated. Benny joined the youth group. He and Jim's daughter, Sharon, were the same age. Jim was furious. He refused to let his daughter go on youth trips. When asked why, his answer was, "I don't want her around him. She might want to date him."

Church members challenged him. "You're not being rational. Your daughter is around this race at school."

His reply, "Church is different. We're more intimate. We talk about God. There's more of a chance of relationships forming. I won't allow it."

Jim's daughter was heartbroken by her father's reaction. She loved God and her church. She also liked Benny. Confused and disillusioned, she rebelled. She became more faithful at church and deliberately cultivated a friendship with Benny. They became best friends and sat together in church. Jim tried to forbid it. He and Sharon had bitter arguments throughout her senior year in high school.

Jim constantly complained about the situation. Fed up, his Sunday School class said, "This is your problem. You have to get over your hate. You are ruining your relationship with Sharon. You are ruining our class." Jim grew angry with the class, and he and his wife left the church. His daughter kept attending.

Today, several years later, Jim lives in a bitter household. He and his wife now argue continually. His son could not wait to move out. Only the daughter is attending church. Jim's health is failing, and he blames it on the stress. His relationship with his daughter is tense and distant. Sharon and Benny never dated, but they remain close friends. Jim blames the church for his difficulties.

"Where is Love? Does it fall from skies above? Is it underneath the willow tree that I've been dreaming of?" (From *Oliver,* "Where is Love"). Don't let prejudice rob you of your ability to love your neighbor as yourself. Instead, be like Peter and say, "God has shown me that no race, religion, creed, or gender is better than another."

CHAPTER 24

Saints, Ain'ts, and Complaints

Praise ye the LORD. Sing unto the LORD a new song, and his praise in the congregation of saints. Let Israel rejoice in him that made him: let the children of Zion be joyful in their King. Let them praise his name in the dance: let them sing praises unto him with the timbrel and harp. For the LORD taketh pleasure in his people: he will beautify the meek with salvation. Let the saints be joyful in glory: let them sing aloud upon their beds. Let the high praises of God be in their mouth, and a two edged sword in their hand; to execute vengeance upon the heathen, and punishments upon the people; to bind their kings with chains, and their nobles with fetters of iron; to execute upon them the judgment written: this honour have all his saints. Praise ye the LORD.

(Ps. 149 KJV)

Driving 23,000 miles is hard on tires, especially when driving on so many dirt roads. On a dry hot day in New Mexico, I was spending it having new tires installed. Fortunately, children filled the Sears waiting room. I brought out my bubble toys, Jesus coloring books, and talking stuffed animals, and we proceeded to play. In this neighborhood, most adults primarily spoke Spanish, so my conversation was limited to the children who could speak both English and Spanish. I contemplated using my junior-high Spanish but laughed at the idea. The most I could say was, "Me llamo es Cheryle" and "No hablo español."

While surrounded by frolicking children trying to catch bubbles, I looked up to see a short, wiry, spry man with deeply etched smile wrinkles. "Can I play?" he asked. He spoke English and Spanish and joined our games. While playing, he kept everyone entertained, as he translated back and forth. I told him about Pocket Full of Quarters. When he translated that to Spanish, everyone looked at me and laughed. Who knows what he said about Pocket Full of Quarters.

As we talked, I discovered he had 7 children and 38 grandchildren. His eldest son gave him 8 of those grandchildren. "You must have taught him how to have a large family," I teased.

"You don't have to be taught that stuff. It comes naturally," was his quick retort.

Knowing he was retired, I asked, "What was your profession?"

"I used to build churches for a living. There are three kinds of Christians you know: Saints, Ain'ts, and Complaints. Which kind are you?"

Saints

Jack sings in the choir, teaches a large Sunday School class, and serves wherever he's needed. One Sunday, a drunken man walked into the service late, disrupting the service with his drunken reverie. He sat down in a front pew, continuing the loud banter. Deacons quickly convened in the back, trying to decide what to do. While their heads were huddled together, Jack got up from his comfortable pew, walked over, and sat beside the man, draping an arm across his shoulder. This smelly dirty creation of God laid his head on Jack's pristine suit and went to sleep. He snored his way through the rest of the service, sleeping peacefully on Jack's shoulder.

The chagrined deacon telling this story said, "Jack acted while the rest of us were still talking. We've never forgotten the lesson of love he taught us."

Ain'ts

The church was in financial trouble and convened an emergency business meeting. "People need to tithe," a deacon loudly exclaimed. "If you're going to attend here, you should be carrying your weight."

Jim spoke up, "It's none of your business how much money anyone gives. Just sit down and be quiet."

Angrily, the deacon (who happened to be Jim's cousin) said, "You just say that because you refuse to give any of your money to the church."

Jim told me this story to explain why he will never go to church again.

Complaints

Susan is an elder in her church. "We're small and won't ever grow. I probably should change churches."

"Why do you say that?" I asked.

"I'm the only spiritual person in the church. No one else has a relationship with God. The preacher is too old to preach on relevant topics. When I suggest topics, he ignores me. We need a new preacher. The leader of the youth group doesn't teach good Bible Study. She fusses at the kids. When I tried to help, she got mad and asked me to leave. I bring up suggestions to our business meetings, and everyone votes against them. I have a doctorate degree, but no one pays any attention to me."

It doesn't seem like someone with a defeatist attitude or a prickly demeanor will be as effective at loving their neighbor as someone who loves and lives like a saint. So, when I think about that man's question, I know what I want my answer to be.

Now it's your turn: Are you a saint, an ain't, or a complaint?

CHAPTER 25

I Need a Baby Jesus

Go ye therefore, and teach all nations, baptizing them in the name of the Father, and of the Son, and of the Holy Ghost; teaching them to observe all things whatsoever I have commanded you; and, lo, I am with you always, even unto the end of the world. Amen.

(Matt. 28:19-20)

A commission is a granting of authority to fulfill certain duties. It is a calling to those duties. Many organizations hold commissioning services for their officers. For example, I served on the board of the Jacksonville Chamber of Commerce. I accepted the position because I cared about business in my city and wanted to help. They commissioned me along with twelve others to act on behalf of the businesses in Jacksonville.

Nervous, I fretted over what to wear. Since I was the only female, there was no one to consult. An evening affair, the usually-safe business suit wasn't appropriate for a woman. I didn't sleep the night before. My only job was to walk up there, raise my right hand at the appropriate time, and say "I do" at the same time everyone else said it.

You think that sounds simple? Think again. I've never been good at looking and acting like other people. Frankly, I would have rather been the guest speaker. They said to raise our right hands, but I raised my left. I was so busy agonizing over the

163

embarrassing motion of lowering my left hand that I missed my one line: "I do." I walked off stage wondering if my commission was valid.

Before Jesus ascended to heaven, he held a commissioning service for His disciples. This commission has been passed down to generations of Christ's disciples ever since. Like my experience with the Jacksonville Chamber, most Christians fumble with their commission.

One woman said, "We sit around at church council meetings and say, 'You know, we really ought to be talking about reaching new Christians.' Then we all look at each other and say, 'Yeah, right,' laugh, and go back to church business." Most churches I visited were only baptizing a few people each year.

One church had made a change. The pastor said, "My heart was broken when I realized that we had only baptized sixteen people the year before. I began to pray. Together, our church developed a heart for reaching people that needed God. Last year, we baptized over a hundred."

I met a couple recovering from alcohol and drug addiction. Together, they have found Jesus Christ. Clean and sober for a year, they are living through all the relationship struggles, hopelessness, and pain that go with a godless past. Their adult children are addicts and/or criminals. Their grandchildren are living in neglect and abuse. Smiling through tears, she said, "We have to live with the consequences of our past, but at least we don't have to do it alone. If we keep showing Jesus to our children, maybe one day they'll find Him, too."

My friend, Sue, was a big part of the Pocket Full of Quarters journey. She read my website daily and even helped with some of the editing. We talked on the phone every few days.

I first met Sue when she was interviewing for a position at my company. I instantly liked her. We worked side by side for several years and became close friends. She is fun, beautiful, and unbelievably loyal to those she loves.

Sue was not always the way she was when I met her. She had a difficult childhood. She grew up in a family that had struggles and addictions. As she became older, she began choosing the path that most of her family chose. This path took her on a long and difficult journey through the hell of addiction. Sue's captivity to alcohol followed the typical pattern. She found herself deep in the dark pit of addiction. Addicts have three choices: death, insanity, or recovery. She chose recovery.

In her pain, she prayed a simple prayer: "Help." God heard and helped. Sue admitted she was powerless over alcohol and that her life was unmanageable. She got the help she needed and became sober. She took her recovery seriously and did what it took to continue, one day at a time. When I met her, she was leading a productive and full life. Despite God's intervention in her life, she was still not willing to believe in Jesus.

Knowing she was not a Christian, I prayed for her daily. *Oh God, lead Sue to the truth. What should my involvement be? Please send others to help.*

God's answer to me was, "Wait for the right time." Being action oriented, waiting is difficult for me. In September of 2000, our company hired a consultant to help with training. That consultant, Karen, went to my church. Karen had just headed up our church's participation in the Billy Graham Crusade. Because of that campaign, her heart was prepared for evangelism. Sue had to work closely with Karen on the work project. Sue liked Karen and mentioned how special and grounded she seemed.

God whispered, "It's time."

"Sue, you are seeing Christ in Karen's life," was all I said. I thanked Karen for being a witness to Sue, and Karen began praying for Sue. During the course of the next year, Sue and I had a few brief conversations about Christ. I let her set the pace. I shudder when I think of the damage pushing could have done. This was my lesson in patience and faith.

Sue had a couple of issues that needed prayer during this time. She asked our church to pray. They were faithful and followed up on her issues. God was faithful and miraculously answered Sue's prayers. One day, Sue came to me beaming, "Your church just called and asked me how my friend was. Wasn't that nice?"

On the morning of September 11, 2001, Sue and I were having work pressures. People were flying in from all over the country for a business planning session. They were all due to arrive at noon. The President of our parent company was on a plane heading to Jacksonville. We saw no way to get everything done. Sue and I were frantic and snapping at each other. Sue looked at me and said, "We need to pray the Serenity Prayer and calm down." I completely agreed.

She shut my office door, and we held hands and prayed together: "God grant us the serenity to accept the things we cannot change, the courage to change the things we can, and the wisdom to know the difference" (The Serenity Prayer).

As we finished praying, someone knocked. "You had better come watch the television." We arrived at the TV in time to see the second of the Twin Towers hit. We stood together stunned and crying. Our company gathered and prayed. People from all religions and beliefs participated in this prayer. Sue and I thought we were praying for "serenity, wisdom, and courage" to host a business planning session. How our perspective changed when the plane hit that building.

As CEO of a subsidiary company, I had my hands full. Because she worked directly with me, Sue had her hands full, too. There were thirty-five people heading to Jacksonville on airplanes. Their families began frantically calling, but we had no answers. Employees had relatives in New York and working in the Pentagon. We had family members of the military working for us. One had a military husband that had shipped out the night before.

All day, we had to deal with the terror of the people around us. We began the process of systematically finding our employees. Praise God that they and their family members were all safe. Most of them spent the day on a grounded airplane.

In the middle of this mayhem, Sue came into my office. Weeping, she said, "This is like Armageddon."

My heart began pounding, a sure sign that God wants something from me. I stopped what I was doing. "Sue, Armageddon is going to be much worse than today." I briefly described it. "Are you ready for it?" I asked.

"I think so," was her hesitant answer.

"Sue, the Bible says you have to believe in Jesus Christ as your Lord and Savior for you to be ready."

She gasped and simply said, "I guess I'm not ready." We went back to work. As bad as things were that day, I knew the conversation with Sue was the most important thing that had happened to me. I wondered if I should say more, but I felt I should leave it alone.

For the next couple of months, Sue and I talked off and on about Christianity. Knowing she was a singer, I invited her to sing in our church's Singing Christmas Tree. To my astonishment and delight, Sue agreed. I prayed for her that Christmas. I hoped singing the words of the Christmas Story would lead her to Christ. I confess to being slightly impatient and discouraged with God's timing. Again, God gently reminded me to trust Him.

Sue loved singing on the tree. The people in the choir fell in love with her and surrounded her with the love of Christ. She was faithful to the choir and an asset to the performance.

Karen had continued praying and was excited that she was singing in the choir. In January 2002, Karen helped start a Seeker's Group at our church. A Seeker's Group is for people seeking God in their life but who have questions. I invited Sue, who seemed interested but noncommittal. Several from the church invited Sue, including Karen. "Are you asking people to call me?" Sue demanded.

I laughed. "You're going to have to blame that on God. You have made your own friends at Southside Baptist Church."

Our Singles Minister, John, introduced himself to Sue. Sue liked him and secretly named him "John, the Baptist." One of the singles in our church, Jan, befriended Sue. John and Jan took Sue to lunch and maintained contact with her. Sue laughed and said, "I'm going to have to join the Seeker's Group. Too many people have invited me." As she participated in the Seeker's Group, her friendship with Karen blossomed. They occasionally met and talked privately. Karen offered prayer and support to Sue throughout this process.

The Seeker's Group took on the challenge of Sue's bold questions. Sue is outspoken and a bit stubborn, yet they didn't judge her. Knowing Sue well, I knew this group had their hands full. Sue struggled with the news that Jesus was the only way to heaven.

"I do not like the idea that a loving God has hell as an option. And how can Jesus be the only way to heaven?"

Finally, Dave, a mature Christian, asked, "What is it that bothers you, Sue? Does it bother you that it is true, or does it bother you that we said it?" Dave was afraid he'd been too firm. Sue has courage and appreciates honesty. She still had difficulty accepting the reality of hell from a loving God, but she courageously continued to seek.

Sue knew God was working in her life because there were too many coincidences. At one point, I realized that Sue did not know the simple "how" of becoming a Christian. She was making it too complicated. I shared with her that all she had to do was to confess her past, believe in Jesus' life, death, and resurrection, and ask Jesus into her life. We talked through the simple plan of salvation. I offered to pray with her when she was ready.

"Thanks for the information," was all she said. I gave her a spiritual tract that had the plan of salvation in it. Sue was amused at how hard I was working not to push.

In April, I lost my job. Sue and I were devastated. We cried together as we grieved about giving up working together. I left on the Pocket Full of Quarters journey. I felt badly leaving Sue in the middle of her seeking, but God was in charge. Sue read the Pocket Full of Quarters website. She talked about the people I was meeting as if they were her friends. She passed my website address around to her friends. She found typing mistakes and offered to fix them.

While I was gone, church members continued to reach out to her. Her friendship with Karen deepened. Sue developed a deep respect for "John, the Baptist," and continued going to the Seeker's Group and asking questions. As I traveled, Sue gave updates on how God was working. She went into a public bathroom, and someone had left a spiritual tract identical to the one I had given her.

One day I said, "Sue, you might as well give up and accept the truth. God is not going to let it rest." She laughed at my impatience.

God is so wonderful. During this process, Sue began dating the man who is now her husband. Rick is a Christian. Early in the dating relationship, Sue asked him, "Do you believe that Jesus Christ is your Lord and Savior?"

His simple answer was, "Absolutely."

When I came back to Jacksonville briefly to celebrate my fiftieth birthday, Sue came to the party and gave me a wonderful present. "When you finish Pocket Full of Quarters, I want to come to your house and ask Jesus into my life."

Again, I was impatient. "Let's do it now."

She smiled. "It will wait. I promise not to die before you get back." I considered cutting my trip short, but Sue said, "And don't try coming home early."

I finished the journey. The day after I returned home, Sue came to my house. We sat on my back porch looking at the moon and the water. She brought her Bible. We walked through the plan of salvation, and Sue marked the scriptures in her Bible. We looked up and saw a rainbow through the light of the moon. She read the Bible aloud, "For God so loved the world that he gave His only begotten Son" (John 3:16).

We came to places where I knew she struggled. Timidly I asked, "Do you believe what you've just read?"

She smiled and said, "Now I understand it. The Seeker's Group explained it. Ray from work also explained one part to me." Sue and I held hands, laughed, and cried as she prayed, "Lord Jesus, come into my life."

The next Thanksgiving, Sue called to say she loved me. "This is my first Thanksgiving as a Christian. I'm grateful for Christ in my life." The next Christmas, Sue sang in The Singing Christmas Tree as a Christian. For the first time, she fully understood the words.

"How is this Christmas different for you?" I asked.

"When I went to put up my Christmas decorations, I realized I had no decorations of the Baby Jesus. I became frantic to get a Baby Jesus. I've found Baby Jesus in my life and needed a Baby Jesus for my Christmas decorations. Rick bought me a Nativity Scene that had a Baby Jesus. This Christmas, I had a Baby Jesus."

Epilogue

Make a joyful noise unto the Lord, all ye lands. Serve the Lord with gladness; come before his presence with singing. Know ye that the Lord he is God; it is he that hath made us, and not we ourselves; we are his people, and the sheep of his pasture. Enter into his gates with thanksgiving, and into his courts with praise; be thankful unto him, and bless his name. For the Lord is good; his mercy is everlasting; and his truth endureth to all generations.

(Ps. 100 KJV)

God blessed me with being able to visit every state in the United States. As I travel through our beautiful country, I meet people making "a joyful noise unto the Lord." America is The Melting Pot because we are a collection of people from all over the world who want to be free to worship God and live the way we think best. In our Pledge of Allegiance we say, "One Nation Under God." The quarters I give away say, "In God We Trust." "We are His people and the sheep of His pasture" (Ps. 100:3 KJV).

I continue to visit churches all over America, and, in almost all, I hear the words, *God is Love*. A worship service is available anytime I seek one. Most churches have programs for the needy as they feed and clothe Jesus by feeding and clothing the "least of his brethren" (Matt. 25:40). They visit Jesus by visiting the sick, the imprisoned, and the distraught. They meet together to worship God the Father, Son, and Holy Ghost, offering a glimpse of the Kingdom of God to those who enter their gates. We "enter into His gates with thanksgiving and into His courts with praise" (Ps. 100:4 KJV).

Then there are the people of America. A man demonstrated his love for Jesus by changing my tire. Another, by following me and telling me I had a low tire. A husband and wife soothed my fears by being sensitive to the voice of God. A Midas franchise owner loved Jesus by repairing my car without charging me. A small girl talked about her love for Jesus as she staked down my tent. People shared their testimonies and made them available to the world through the web. I was overwhelmed by the people that "served Him with gladness" (Ps. 100:2 KJV).

There is so much to be grateful for in America. Our landscape is magnificent. I worshiped God by all five of the Great Lakes. I've lost count of the number of prayers I've had by waterfalls cascading down sides of mountains. We have City, State, and National Parks throughout our nation, preserved for our prayer time and enjoyment. We can grow our faith beside Old Faithful in Yellowstone National Park or let our Presidents inspire us at Mt. Rushmore.

We can swim in the warm relaxing oceans of Florida or the cooler refreshing oceans of California. We can stand gazing at the orange, gold, and red plunging Grand Canyon and witness God's splendor by the hoodoos in Bryce Canyon. As I worshiped throughout our country, I knew that "the Lord He is God; it is He that has made us and not we ourselves" (Ps. 100:3 KJV).

Do we Americans love God with all of our mind, heart, soul, and strength? Do we love our neighbors as ourselves? I met a woman broken before God by her own alcoholism who now spends her life trying to help others. "Most don't make it, but every once in a while, one person makes it all worthwhile." The couple that travels America planting churches says, "This is the greatest life we could have." The answer to the question of love is that many are trying to "come into His presence with singing."

Is America perfect? No, is the only answer one can render. People are starving and wandering our streets. There are those that hate God and—despite the effectiveness of 12-Step Programs—we have addicts still practicing their disease. I visited cold and godless churches where no one spoke to me. I met a couple that hated America and was moving to a different country.

A man said, "I will not discuss God with you or anyone." He went on to give friendly suggestions about the area. I talked with numerous people that had been sexually or physically abused by a trusted family or clergy member. Many were overwhelmed, frustrated, and exhausted by the chaos, noise, and abundance of living the American Dream. Our nation has problems but "His mercy is everlasting."

What is the answer to our problems? I propose to you that the answer is the *Sh'ma*.

Thou shalt love the Lord thy God with all thy heart, and with all thy soul, and with all thy strength, and with all thy mind; and thy neighbour as thyself.

(Luke 10:27 KJV)

The *Sh'ma* is the answer to every single problem I have witnessed while handing out quarters. When we stop working on our problems and begin working on the *Sh'ma*, we find the answer to all that we seek.

After meeting so many people and listening to so many stories and after studying the lives of the disciples, I have found the following pattern to be an excellent way to live out the *Sh'ma* in our lives:

Step 1 – Follow God, mind to Mind
Step 2 – Please God, heart to Heart
Step 3 – Embrace God, soul to Soul
Step 4 – Serve God, strength by Strength
Step 5 – Love God's Children, neighbor to neighbor

Some reject stepping onto this not-so-secret ladder. They end up spending their lives wondering what is wrong. Some take one or two steps and stand frozen, wondering why their faith is unfulfilling. Most continually go up and down this ladder of spiritual growth, as we take one step forward and two steps backwards. Occasionally, we fall off the ladder completely. The wonder of God's grace is that we can always climb back on the ladder to begin our progress upward towards peace and happiness beyond our wildest dreams. Let us dedicate our lives to the journey of falling in love with God, always making a "joyful noise before the Lord" because "His truth endures for all generations."

Sources

Dictionary.com, Lexico Publishing Group LLC

Mr. Rogers' Neighborhood song "Won't You Be My Neighbor," composer Fred M. Rogers

The Wizard of Oz songs: "If I Only Had the Nerve," "If I Only Had a Brain," "If I Only Had a Heart," lyrics by E. H. Harburg, music by Harold Arlene

The Broadway Musical *Oliver* song "Where is Love," words and original music by Lionel Bart

Bibles:

The King James Version
The New International Version
The Message
The Amplified Version
New American Standard Bible

To order additional copies of

POCKET FULL OF
Quarters

Have your credit card ready and call:

1-877-421-READ (7323)

Please visit our web site at
www.pleasantword.com

Also available at:
www.pocketfullofquarters.com
www.amazon.com
www.barnesandnoble.com

The author, Cheryle M. Touchton, would be honored to speak at your church or organization. To contact her, call 1-904-821-5207 or e-mail *Cheryle@pocketfullofquarters.com*. Photographs from the Pocket Full of Quarters journey may be enjoyed on the companion website *www.pocketfullofquarters.com*

CPSIA information can be obtained at www.ICGtesting.com

225173LV00002BA/221/A